Outsiders in
Urban Societies

DAVID SIBLEY

Outsiders in Urban Societies

St. Martin's Press · New York

Printed in Great Britain

First published in the United States of America in 1981

Library of Congress Card Catalog Number 81-9292

ISBN 0-312-59192-6

Contents

Preface

An understanding of gypsies and indigenous minorities in advanced capitalist societies requires involvement in their day-to-day lives, but the intimate knowledge that might be gained from such contact is in itself insufficient if we are concerned with explaining the peripheral status of these communities in relation to the larger society. In order to obtain an appropriate perspective on the problem, it is necessary to look at changes in the economy and social structure of the outsider group as they are affected by processes operating in the dominant social system. Beyond this fairly obvious requirement, our understanding may be increased by repeating the analysis on an international and cross-cultural basis, since this should enable us to isolate elements of the problem that are peculiar to certain societies. Such a comparative framework is used in this book.

The title of the book is not intended to suggest a particular academic focus, and I have made a conscious attempt to cross disciplinary boundaries because an account of the problem solely from an economic, anthropological, or some other customary academic perspective could be limiting. Those aspects of life that constitute 'the outsider problem' — the social, economic and political dimensions — are clearly intertwined, and the interaction of these elements needs to be considered if we are to avoid a one-dimensional characterization of peripheral communities. The context of the study is probably best summarized by the term 'social formation', since this suggests the structuring of economic behaviour and social action by ideology, and it is the ideological aspect of the problem that is given particular emphasis.

My primary interest is in gypsies and other peripheral groups in urban areas, because it is in the city that conflict is most acute and where the presence of a non-conforming minority is most likely to be a political issue — there is the possibility of confrontations involving large numbers of people, and this can be of electoral significance at the local level. Urban problems are a rather arbitrary concern in some respects, however, because most of the rural population in industrialized countries has strong urban connections and certainly cannot be distinguished from urban communities in its response to outsiders. Thus, it would be reasonable to look at the social formation as a whole rather just the urban part of it; at least, this provides a justification for considering manifestations of the outsider problem in rural or peripheral regions, particularly in relation to indigenous populations, without having to abandon the essentials of my theoretical argument. It remains the case, however, that the issues are primarily urban ones.

The bulk of the book, in its concern with British gypsies, concentrates on problems at the local level, like much anthropological research. If this part of the work were to be allocated to a conventional methodological pigeon-hole, it could conceivably be represented as a product of participant observation, but this would be misleading. My contact with travelling people over a nine-year period has been not in the role of a research worker but, a few years of political activism apart, has been an informal, social association involving my family rather than me as an individual. Initially, there was no deliberate and considered research strategy; a potentially useful research problem occurred to me only after several years of contact. Certain benefits derive from the nature of the contact, however. In particular, knowledge comes from unsolicited comment rather than from responses to pointed questions, while, reflecting on many conversations and incidents, it has been possible to resolve some of the contradictions that appear in travellers' attitudes to the larger society and to individual outsiders, like myself, with whom they have a social relationship. This has been an essentially local experience and I have tried to enlarge on it, first, by examining the association between travellers and cities on a national basis, in Britain and elsewhere, and then by looking for parallels and contrasts in the relationship between the dominant society and indigenous minorities, particularly native Americans.

Several sections of the book deal with the state's response to outsiders and this involves a critical examination of ostensibly benevolent social policies. From my discussion of the actions of the state, however, it should be clear that I make no distinction between practice and theory. Social science theories are ideological and practice is informed by ideology; the way in which the dominant groups in society perceive and manipulate others depends upon their beliefs about the proper constitution of social life. Thus, in an attempt to convey the idea of the interconnection of ideology, theory and practice, these topics are discussed together rather than exclusively. Simply to inject some order into the discussion, I start with chapters that are largely theoretical and set the problem up, and proceed to describe the traveller economy, the relationship between British gypsies and the state, and the urban dimension of the problem, both historically and cross-culturally. I then look elsewhere to consider the state—minority relationship in the North American Arctic before returning briefly to consider the relevance of my arguments to certain social groups in the larger society; but all these substantive accounts are accompanied by theoretical asides.

My intellectual debts are many, but I have been strongly influenced by two writers who have had a considerable influence on each other: the social anthropologist Mary Douglas, and Basil Bernstein. In my enthusiasm for their arguments I have probably neglected contrary views, but I am impressed by the generality of their theories and both are helpful in exposing the connection between social problems and spatial problems. On the question of the state's response to outsiders, Frank Parkin's critique of Marx's class analysis convinces me, and I find a close similarity between this argument and the conclusions reached by John Berger in his study of the peasant in industrial society. I have used these writers to support my own ideological position, which is essentially an anarchist one. There is an anarchistic thread running through the book, but I have not developed the argument at any length, partly because it did not seem appropriate to do so in a study that is partly empirical, and also because I am not entirely convinced by anarchist theory. However, as a result of my involvement with travelling people, I feel that state involvement with peripheral minorities is highly damaging, and that the position of these communities in a society where the state's role is reduced or minimized warrants critical consideration.

Acknowledgements

Apart from the travelling people who were the inspiration for this work, I am grateful to a number of people for their assistance. The library staff of the Scott Polar Research Institute, Cambridge, directed me to many sources on the native peoples of the North American Arctic, and the University of Hull provided financial assistance for this research. The diagrams were skilfully drawn by Keith Scurr and Derek Waite of the Department of Geography, Hull University. I have benefited from numerous conversations with other people working with travellers, but I am particularly indebted to Megan Edwards, for her understanding of travelling people and her encouragement.

A note on terminology

In referring to ethnic minorities, I have generally used self-ascriptions. Thus, British gypsies are identified as 'travellers' or 'travelling people' rather than gypsies because 'gypsy', like 'tinker', 'caravan dweller' and 'itinerant', is used in a pejorative sense by members of the settled society in Britain. I have not been entirely consistent, however, and I occasionally use 'gypsy' as an alternative to 'traveller' simply for variety. Following the same principle, I refer to the North American Eskimos as the 'Inuit' and occasionally use 'Dene' as a term for Canadian Indians. Several words and expressions from the speech of British travellers appear in the text — I describe non-gypsies as *gaujes* (alternatively, *gorgios* or *gajes*), caravans as 'trailers' and unofficial sites as 'stopping places'.

CHAPTER 1

Incidents

A small number of travelling families were camped in a lane on the edge of a village in the north of England. It was July and the families had recently returned to this stopping place after a spell of farm work which was a regular event in the seasonal pattern of work and migration. The annual cycle of movement had changed little in the past ten years, but finding places on the roadside to camp could be a problem as old stopping places were being built over or closed off with banks of earth. This lane was a good place to pull in for several reasons. It was away from the houses but close enough to the village for a walk to the shop; the grass verge was wide — it could accommodate a wagon or a trailer and it provided enough grazing for the horses; there was no traffic down the lane apart from the occasional tractor so it was safe for the children to play in and the travellers were ignored most of the time. In this respect, it was unlike the outskirts of the city, where families were frequently moved on by council officials and the police. One other attraction of this lane was its nearness to a refuse tip. When a lorry would drive on to the tip, someone would shout, and as the lorry emptied its load of household refuse, men, women and children from the camp could run on to the tip and search through the garbage for anything useful. This could be unpleasant work, particularly in summer when there was a strong smell of rotting food and a lot of flies, but at the same time it could be quite profitable. It was common to find discarded items containing metal that could be separated and sold for scrap, and, when there was no farm work available and not much return from hawking

1

goods round the villages, this was a useful source of income. The
council workers did not object — in fact, the bin men and the
travellers ignored each other.

There was, however, one local council officer who was determined to make life difficult for the travellers. He could, for
example, use his powers under the 1936 Public Health Act, which
had made it an offence to disturb material on a refuse tip because
of the potential danger to health. One afternoon, while some of
the travellers were sorting through material on the tip, the man
from the council arrived in the company of two police officers.
His intention was to serve a summons for contravening the Public
Health Act and the police came along to reinforce his authority.
Things did not go smoothly, however. When they confronted the
travellers there was an argument; a woman was pushed by the
council official and a fight ensued, involving the woman's husband,
one of her sons and the police. Alarmed by what was happening,
several other people from the same family ran on to the tip to give
some support and the police called up reinforcements. More police
arrived with dogs and surrounded the camp, but four of the men
who had been involved in the fight hid in the trailers and then
escaped into a cornfield pursued by police dog-handlers. That
afternoon they eluded the police, who eventually gave up the
hunt. Several days later, however, two men were arrested after a
dawn raid on the camp; one was held on remand in prison and the
other sent to a detention centre for young offenders.

When they were first brought to the local magistrate's court, the
police opposed bail on the grounds that they were gypsies and
therefore, they claimed, likely to move out of the area. Bail was
refused and both men were brought to trial three weeks later.
They were charged with grievous bodily harm. It transpired during
the prosecution's evidence, however, that one of the police officers
suffered only slight damage to his wrist which kept him off work
for two days while the other had a bruised buttock and was otherwise unharmed. The charge was then reduced to the lesser one of
actual bodily harm. At one point in the hearing, one of the police-
men, who had known the travellers for several years, tried to argue
that there were aggravating circumstances, particularly the provo-

cative behaviour of the council official, and he stressed the close family ties of the travellers which contributed to their highly emotional response to the official's actions. However, he was told by the prosecuting solicitor that sympathetic comment was out of place and that he was required only to give a factual account of the afternoon's events. Both men were found guilty and fined £80 each, with an additional sum to cover the cost of a new watch for one of the officers, who had lost it during the fight. A large number of relatives of the accused were in court. Together, they collected enough money to pay the fines, and the police and the gypsies parted on reasonably friendly terms.

Eight gypsy families are gradually being encircled with refuse dumped by York Corporation in an attempt to move them from a former caravan site. A council official admitted that the tipping was a deliberate policy, but he said that the refuse was first incinerated and was not a health risk to the gypsies or their children. However, the gypsies — who are refusing to leave the Love Lane site until a new one is ready for them at a disused aerodrome on the outskirts of York — claim that the refuse contains rotting tomatoes and the remains of dead pets and that the smell is intolerable after rain. Residents nearby, who in the past have been critical of gypsies, are also concerned about the council's tactics.

A spokesman for the Corporation said that it was a long-standing policy to clear the site and tipping was part of that policy. 'If you don't tip, you will get more gypsies,' he said.

[*The Guardian*, 4 October 1975]

A secret squad of hired workmen, backed by police, evicted gypsies from sites in Sheffield today. The dawn raid, by workmen driving vans, Landrovers and excavators, took the gypsies by surprise. Eight families were moved from sites in Selborne Street, Cottingham Street and Chelmsford Street, Attercliffe. The workmen had been hired from a firm of private contractors and one of the conditions was that the firm's identity should be kept a secret. The Attercliffe operation was organized by Mr Roger Pensam, head of the council's legal department. He said, 'I'm pleased with the way today's operation has gone. The tinkers have been warned on a number of occasions and we have given them the opportunity to move themselves. They are trespassing and it is our duty to move them.'

[*The Star* (Sheffield), 17 August 1979]

CHAPTER 2

Outsiders in an economic and political perspective

Groups are identified as outsiders because their social structures and economies are perceptibly different from those of the larger society. They are peripheral in the sense that there is a considerable social distance between them and the majority — there is little or no social interaction — and this social gulf is usually, but not necessarily, reinforced by spatial separation. It will not be possible to provide an adequate account of outsider status, however, by paying exclusive attention to differentiating characteristics. It is just as important to analyse the structure of the dominant social systems to which some minorities have a tenuous attachment, to describe the contours of the larger society, as Cohen (1980) puts it, since, to a large degree, it is the dominant society that creates outsiders. This gives the study of small minorities some wider significance; for, by getting beyond the dominant system and assessing it from the perspective of an excluded minority, it may be possible to view the structure of the larger society in a more critical light. As Marchand (1979) has remarked, 'a black ghetto is the place to study the defects of white society'.

In reviewing alternative conceptions of social groups as outsiders, I will work in this chapter towards what I believe to be a correct interpretation of their status. By this, I mean that I will try to identify a model that tallies closely with my own experience. On the way, however, I will discuss the ideological basis of alternative viewpoints which entails looking at changing attitudes

4

towards peripheral groups and at attitudes that we can attribute to different interests in mainstream society — politicians, industrialists, researchers and so on.

Two conceptions of outsiders that are virtually polar opposites might provide a useful starting point for discussion, namely imperialist and Marxist views. The first is conventionally associated with the nineteenth-century tradition of colonial or imperialist anthropology but it is manifest also in present-day attitudes to minorities.[1] Tribal societies in colonial territories were described in exotic terms, with particular emphasis on aspects of physical or cultural differentiation, which had the effect of dehumanizing them. Descriptions and cultural artefacts of tribes constituted part of the wealth extracted by colonial regimes from distant territories. It is not entirely fair, however, to portray nineteenth-century European anthropologists as instruments of colonial regimes, insensitive to the exploitation of tribal societies. Sir Richard Burton, for example, writing about the Fan in West Africa, was highly critical of the white merchants who traded with the local population. As he commented: 'May the day come when unanimity will enable the West African merchants to abstain from living upon the lives of those who pour wealth into their coffers' (Penzer, 1924).[2]

In general, however, this interest in 'foreign' cultures contributed to the formation of romantic and ethnocentric stereotypes that have persisted — debates on gypsies in the British Parliament, for example, demonstrate the relevance of the imperialist tradition to current attitudes. The danger of this characterization of peripheral groups is that, while they may be considered exotic and interesting at a distance, they become deviant when enmeshed in the social mainstream because of the hegemony of the dominant value system. Thus, Guthrie, commenting on research on the indigenous population of Australia, asserts that:

---

1 For a criticism of this approach, see Goddard (1972).
2 Wendy James (1973) claims that 'the very existence of social anthropology in the colonial period constituted a source of potential radical criticism of the colonial order itself'.

Academic research has been so dominantly anthropological [sic] that it
appears that more is known about the cultures of traditional Aborigines than
about current Aboriginal cultures. European involvement in Aboriginal affairs
has also seen a greater concern for Aborigines in more distant parts of Australia.
Perhaps it is easier to be moralistic on behalf of people one never meets; perhaps it is because these people better fit the white image of blacks as an out-
back group. [Guthrie, n.d.] [3]

Where outsiders come into close physical association with the
larger society, particularly in cities, the romantic image, the per-
vasive myth about minority culture, is retained as a yardstick
against which outsiders are measured. Experience of the minority
at first hand contradicts the myth but it does not explode it. The
myth can be retained because failure to meet mythical expectations is attributed to deviancy or to social pathologies that are
somehow a product of urban living.

The principal alternative to the imperialist argument I have
called a Marxist one, although it has been advanced also by academics who are not Marxists but who might be pigeon-holed as
'liberal' or 'left-wing'. In this analysis, the processes of domination
and integration in advanced capitalist societies are represented as
irresistible forces, and peripheral status is seen as a transitional
condition between cultural autonomy and full incorporation into
the class system, with resultant cultural annihilation.

This argument has its appeal, given the evident poverty of peripheral groups in advanced capitalist societies and from observations on the impact of technology and industrial organization on
societies formerly dependent on hunting, gathering and trading. I
would suggest, however, that it is simplistic. There are variations in

---

3 Guthrie's use of 'anthropological' here clearly implies the imperialist type
of ethnography and cannot be taken as a characterization of anthropological research in general. There is an interesting parallel to the shift in
attitude to outsiders from 'exotic' to 'deviant' that accompanies their incorporation into the dominant system, in the changing response to criminal deviancy. Maguire (1974) suggests that the Lombrosian myth about
'criminal types' has given way to a 'like us, essentially, but . . .' attitude.
The latter implies a need for rehabilitation to fit the recidivist for society,
and this is characteristically an element of official policy towards peripheral ethnic minorities.

the relationship between the dominant society and groups commonly considered to be marginal which suggest that an explanation couched solely in terms of the requirements of the capitalist mode of production would be inadequate. In particular, there are differences in the degree of autonomy or dependency that can be related to historical materialist views only with difficulty. Reconciliation of the class system with the autonomy of some outsider groups requires some rather clever argument. I will maintain in this chapter that we need to unravel the relative contributions of industrial interests, the state, and the economy of peripheral groups themselves in creating and maintaining peripheral status, and that any analysis requires a certain amount of theoretical eclecticism. I am sceptical about global theories, first, because there are differences between peripheral groups in regard to traditional forms of economic organization; second, because the political dimension of the relationship between peripheral groups and dominant interests varies; and, third, because the cultures of outsider groups have both exposed and hidden elements that render any analysis ambiguous. Initially, however, we can consider the essentials of the historial materialist case.

In an explanation of their present status, the operations of capitalism may be of overwhelming importance for some groups, as Jorgensen has suggested in discussing the urban Indian in North America. Thus, he asserts that:

Underdevelopment ... has been caused by the development of the white-controlled national economy, and the political, economic and social conditions of the Indian are not improving because the American Indian is, and has been for over one hundred years, fully integrated into the national political economy. Underdevelopment, paradoxically [sic] then, has been caused by the development of the capitalist political economy of the United States. [Jorgensen, 1971]

This rather naive realization of the role of capital in the creation of peripheral status has been stated with greater conviction by others. Of primary importance are the expansionary forces accompanying the accumulation process. Marcuse (1977), for example, has observed that accumulation is an imperative of the capitalist mode of production; Harvey (1975) has called accumulation 'the engine which powers growth under the capitalist mode of production. The capitalist system is therefore highly dynamic and inevitably expansionary.' Harvey recognizes the conditions for accumulation as the existence of a surplus of labour that includes 'latent elements', such as women and ethnic minorities, and markets for production and consumption. Market expansion can be effected either by the intensification of existing markets within a spatial structure, for example by creating a demand for new products, or by territorial expansion of the market, or both. If an economy expands spatially to increase production through the exploitation of industrial resources, in order to secure investments, it becomes necessary to eliminate competing claims to land and other resources from the indigenous populations in peripheral territories, such as the Northern Territories of Australia, Arctic Canada, Alaska and the Soviet Arctic. This may be achieved by making territorial concessions and by involving native communities in the political process — strategies that legitimate the appropriation of resources — and by the incorporation of the indigenous population in the workforce. A consequence of the development of extractive industries in peripheral regions is that the traditional mode of production is disrupted, dependence on occasional wage labour and welfare is increased, and the native population assumes a lumpenproletarian status. This is the 'metropolitan dominance' or 'internal colonialism' thesis in regard to core—periphery relationships, and it is not difficult to marshall convincing evidence in support of the argument.

Much of the development that affects indigenous minorities in peripheral regions involves a liaison between capital and the state, and particular problems arise in defining the role of the state in the processes of accumulation and incorporation. In Western, industrialized societies, the state is ostensibly concerned with the welfare of minorities, intervening in the market to provide housing, medical services, special education and employment training programmes. Thus, government policies might be seen to act in opposition to capital, the latter being primarily responsible for the exploitation of peripheral groups. A number of Marxist writers, however, see the state and capital as indivisible. Miliband (1969), for example, recognizes an ideological consensus, with state and capital working hand in hand in the accumulation process.[4] Since accumulation necessarily involves the exploitation of the working class, if it is not to antagonize exploited groups the state must provide them with some tangible benefits in order to distract them from those actions that run counter to working-class interests. Further, the provision made for the working class only confirms their class position and contributes to the reproduction of the class society rather than to its transformation — council housing in Britain, for example, serves this function. The state might occasionally demonstrate its autonomy by acting against capital, but government and capitalist interests are generally coincident. This is suggested, for example, by the Canadian government's role in the development of the industrial resources of the Arctic. Large subsidies have been provided to companies engaged in the exploitation of oil, gas and other mineral reserves on the grounds that the development of the North is in the national interest; in fact, is an economic and political imperative. By contrast, the social provision made for the native peoples of the Arctic to mitigate the disruptive effects of industrial development has involved the allocation of very little public money.

Apart from providing favourable conditions for capital investment, the state is concerned with ensuring an adequate supply of labour, which requires a number of regulatory activities, including, according to Mingione (1972), town planning. He argues that the 'segregation, differentiation and a hierarchic organization of space utilization' are characteristics of town planning that serve the interests of dominant groups, such as industrialists and property speculators but, at the same time, restrict the opportunities of the working class and reinforce its class position. This argument has particular force in relation to the state's treatment of peripheral groups.

To summarize, the materialist argument would be that accumu-

---

4 For a detailed assessment of alternative views of the role of the state in capitalist social formations, see Koch (1980).

lation is an imperative of the capitalist mode of production; this may require territorial expansion of industrial capital in order to harness industrial resources; if this process creates conflict between capital and an indigenous population, the state will defuse the conflict by making some provision for the exploited class. This provision, however, is only a means of legitimating the activities of capital, with which the state can be identified, since, by supporting capital, politicians can secure their own dominant role in society. In order to make its activities appear legitimate to those groups whose interests are basically antagonistic to those of capital, the state has to 'conceal the power relations that are the basis of its force' (Bourdieu and Passeron, 1977) by dressing up its policies in such a way that they appear to represent social justice for the exploited. In passing, it is worth pointing out that terms like 'modernization', used in relation to peripheral ethnic groups, endow the legitimation process with academic respectability. Entry to the social mainstream is seen as both desirable and inevitable rather than being a process of securing permanent exploitation as the minority loses its autonomy and assumes lumpenproletarian status.

There are a number of problems with this thesis that are relevant to any structuralist analysis of peripheral status. First, there is the question of the state's liaison with capital which is particularly problematic at the local level. Pahl (1977), for example, maintains that there is a local 'urban technostructure' that operates in important respects independently of economic interests. It could be argued that local administrations have become technically sophisticated, with efficiency, order and control taking priority over specific social or economic considerations. Elected representatives may find the advice of officers compelling because it is couched in technical terms and sounds authoritative, and in this way the technocracy gains influence. However, administrative methods, using systems analysis, for example, have ideological underpinnings that are consistent with the interests of the dominant groups in society (Sayer, 1976), so it is unlikely that the local state apparatus will exercise control over social groups in any way that conflicts with the interests of capital. As a possible illustration of this, it appears that some Labour-controlled councils in Britain adopt policies that are heavily influenced by the techno-cracy, and these policies work against the interests of the working class, for example in pursuing a programme of slum clearance and rehousing with few or no resources directed to the rehabilitation of older property.[5] Similarly, in relation to government policy for gypsies in England and Wales, we can recognize an ideology of control that does not vary with the political complexion of the local authority but is generally in harmony with the interests of capital. The urban managers do not appear to have an entirely independent role in the urban political economy.

The second problem concerns the relationship of peripheral groups to the working class. So far, I have not suggested that the identification of outsiders with the working class is problematic and, in Marxist terms, it is a necessary connection. Difficulties arise, however, when we have to explain phenomena such as con-flict between a working-class majority and ethnic minorities. Racist organizations like the Ku Klux Klan and the National Front have strong white working-class support, and it is a notable feature of conflicts between gypsies and the settled community in Britain that Labour councils and working-class residents can be particu-larly hostile; two of the most repressive city councils in Britain — Swansea and Sheffield — are Labour-controlled. If the working class is to embrace the excluded minority, then conflict between workers and groups distinguished by their ethnicity, who presum-ably qualify for membership of the working class on economic grounds, must be put down to false consciousness. The majority sees the ethnic minority as a threat to its own share of material wealth — housing, jobs and so on — and so turns against it, but this conflict is generated by the exploitation of the working class in general: 'any given set of closure strategies (that is, strategies to exclude a social minority) could in principle be understood as mere responses to the material pressures and forces set in play by

---

5 Pahl (1979) has suggested that authoritarian approaches to resource alloca-tion are more likely in long-standing Labour-controlled councils in Britain than in Conservative ones.

the capitalist mode of production' (Parkin, 1979). However, as Parkin argues in a criticism of the Marxist view,

This serious lack of fit between all positional or systemic definitions of class and the actual behaviour of classes in the course of distributive struggle, is due not to any lack of refinement in the categories employed. It arises from the initial theoretical decision to discount the significance and effect of the cultural and social make-up of the groups assigned to the categories in question. Models constructed upon such formal, systemic definitions require of their advocates much ingenuity in accounting for *the continuous and whole-sale discrepancies between class behaviour* [my emphasis]. [Parkin, 1979]

Parkin cites the practice of apartheid in South Africa in support of his case. I will argue that there are cultural, including economic, characteristics of peripheral groups like gypsies and the native peoples of the North American Arctic that distinguish their interests from those of the working-class majority: there is a real cleavage that cannot be explained away as false consciousness on the part of different fractions of the working class.

A third problem with an analysis that is concerned exclusively with the capitalist mode of production and purports to explain peripheral status in terms of class conflict in that social formation is that the same process of exploitation and incorporation is characteristic of other modes of production. In this connection, it is interesting to read Gurvich's (1978) account of the ethnic minority problem in Siberia. He suggests that socialist transformations of peripheral groups involve 'dramatic changes in languages, accompanied by the disappearance of dialects; the liquidation of tribal structure, ... the supplanting of tribal and local forms of identification by national forms; and the incorporation of small, separate ethnic groups into the bulk of the nation'. This devaluation of traditional culture and belief in the benefits of incorporation in the dominant system is directly comparable to the capitalist view of peripheral groups — in the Canadian Arctic, for example: it is equally totalitarian.

What unifies capitalist and socialist systems in their response to peripheral groups is a belief in progress or an inevitable change to a mature state where the path of change is clearly mapped out and is inherent in the political system. This is what Giddens (1979) has termed 'an unfolding model of social change' (ch. 6). This model, which an anthropologist like Gurvich would presumably be happy with, can be contrasted with one that locates social change in sources external to the system, where tradition is dominant in social reproduction (Giddens, 1979, citing Nisbet, 1969). Thus, the conflict between dominant cultures and peripheral cultures might be seen as a conflict between these two models rather than as one between capital and a working class of which peripheral groups form a part. Given the manifest similarity in the status of indigenous minorities in capitalist and socialist states, an explanation that gets beyond the confines of the capitalist mode of production is required.

AN ALTERNATIVE CONCEPTION OF OUTSIDERS

A restatement and amplification of Giddens's observations on social change can be found in John Berger's (1979b) work on the historical experience of European peasantry[6] and this provides a convenient link between the previous and ensuing discussions. Berger's analysis is useful because it points to the essential difference in world-view between the dominant society and outsiders and provides a basis for comparing the structure of alternative world-views. He makes a distinction between cultures of progress and cultures of survival. Cultures of progress envisage ever-expanding horizons — the imperative of accumulation — and they may be capitalist or socialist: 'The struggle between capitalism and socialism is, at an ideological level, a fight about the content of progress, not about its necessity.' Marx's observation that Western capitalism was engaged in a restless drive towards expansion and had a corroding effect upon traditional cultures (Giddens, 1979) could be applied equally to the Soviet system. Berger then defines a culture of survival as one that 'envisages the future as a sequence of repeated acts for survival. Each act pushes a thread through the eye of a needle and the thread is tradition.' This conception of continuity and adaptation to externally induced change in order to ensure cultural survival sets peasant or peripheral group culture

---

6 His analysis appears in the Historical Afterword, pp. 195–213.

apart from the culture of the dominant capitalist or socialist systems, and it implies the existence of a cultural boundary that
serves to absorb or deflect pressures exerted by the larger society.
In particular, economic self-sufficiency, as a fact or an objective,
separates the peasantry from the class system and helps the
peasant to resist incorporation. Berger asserts that the undeclared
relation of the peasant tradition to the dominant class culture was
often heretical and subversive.

This analysis is clearly incompatible with one that locates all
outsider groups in the dominant system as part of either the
residual or active labour force. Berger's argument is equally applicable to semi-nomadic cultures like gypsies that maintain their
autonomy by adapting to the dominant culture. They have a
tenuous and spasmodic attachment to the wage labour system,
but, otherwise, travelling people have successfully stayed apart
from the larger society *because* that society provides their economic base. As Gmelch (1977b) has put it, the economic resources
of travellers are social rather than physical, and they are urban
rather than rural; it is the nature of the social relationship between
gypsies and the dominant system that provides the clues to the
former's autonomy. The economic independence of travelling
people is continually reaffirmed by their world-structure, that is,
their conception of society, which is shaped by routine encounters
within the group and reinforced by the experience of dealing with
people outside the community. The term suggests a distinctive
categorical system and, thus, a distinctive interpretation of social
life. They have succeeded in maintaining a boundary between
themselves and the larger society that assists in exploiting opportunities created by the dominant system. From within the bounded
world of the traveller, the house-dweller is seen as both polluting
and exploitable. This requires the traveller to assume a dominant
position in economic transactions with the settled community and
to maintain a social distance in order to avoid pollution. The
fundamental nature of the barrier erected by gypsies to ensure cultural survival is implied by the Romany word for non-gypsy, *gauje*
(alternatively *gorgio* or *gaje*), which literally means 'stranger' but
implies a threat; the capacity to pollute.

This is the basis of resistance to the capitalist or socialist mode of production. We could assert that any social formation that recognizes that its tradition sets it apart from the dominant system will try to maintain and reproduce itself by excluding threatening elements, characteristically by ritual taboo, in contrast to the dominant society, which uses legal sanctions to exclude ethnic minorities. Thus, the gypsies' rejection of activities, social relationships or objects as *mochadi* or *marime,* that is, unclean, is instrumental in retaining their cultural integrity. Gypsies constitute a clear case of a culture that is within but outside the dominant system; indigenous minorities that have a traditionally land-based economy, like the Inuit (Eskimo) in the North American Arctic, might be considered more vulnerable to the expansionary force of capitalism, but they too have an economy that is to some extent obscured from the view of the larger society and provides a similar basis for autonomy. Since the dominant society is largely unaware of the existence of this economy, it is difficult to manipulate.

To polarize the argument, suggesting incorporation and autonomy as alternative destinies for peripheral cultures, opposing Marxist class divisions and ethnic social cleavages, distorts the picture. In fact, domination and economic independence are both characteristic tendencies of outsider cultures — they overlap to different degrees in specific cultural situations. To suggest that English gypsies, for example, are an autonomous group on the boundary of mainstream society is an idealistic conception that ignores the power relationship between gypsy and non-gypsy, and it is a view that becomes increasingly inappropriate as state control of the activities of travellers increases.[7] Conversely, the native peoples of the Canadian Arctic may have a greater capacity for self-reliance than is commonly assumed. It is unreasonable to be categorical on this issue. Similarly, in assessing the constraints on the activities of peripheral groups that result from government

---

7 This is an overstatement. As the chapters on the official response to travelling people will demonstrate, there are indications of increasing dependence on the larger society but also of continuing autonomy, and the contradiction cannot be resolved on the basis of evidence that is very limited in time and space.

policies, it is necessary to make qualifications. The desire of the dominant society to control both non-conforming groups and their activities through the agency of the urban technocracy may be a general one, but society's success in achieving this goal varies. Both the need for control and the possibility of exercising control differ according to the degree to which outsider groups are hidden, or manifestly non-conforming, and, related to this, according to the adaptive possibilities presented by the built environment. Gypsies in England, for example, are much more conspicuous than gypsies in the United States, more of a political issue and subject to greater control, principally because of differences in the housing market and in the organization of social space that affect adaptive opportunities.

MUTED GROUPS

John Berger refers to peasants as a class apart. We can examine the proposition that social groups like peasants are differentiated from the urban majority by their world-structure and by the relationship of their perception of experience to that of the larger society. One way of conceptualizing the problem has been suggested by Charlotte Hardman (1973), who has described groups that are in some senses detached from the social mainstream as 'muted groups', mutedness suggesting that they are partly hidden within the social structure because of a communication barrier. As Ardener (1975) explains this, a group is muted 'simply because it does not form part of the dominant communicative system of the society — expressed as it must be through the dominant ideology and that mode of production . . . which is articulated with it'. Ardener applies this model to the problem of the domination of women in society, but, equally, we could fit into this scheme other groups whose needs are not articulated in the dominant world-structure for economic reasons and/or because they do not communicate in the idiom of the dominant group, such as mentally ill or old people.

Ardener represents the problem graphically as a Venn diagram

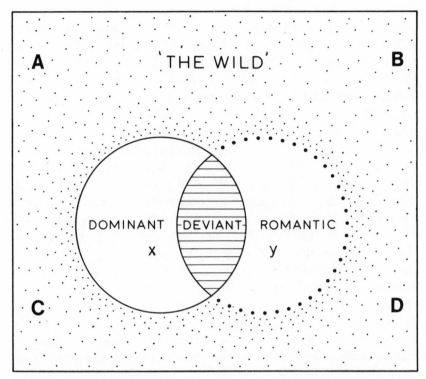

Figure 1   The relationship between dominant and muted groups.
(After Ardener, 1975)

situated in an unbounded field (figure 1). In the diagram, x and y
are the world-structures of the dominant and muted groups,
respectively. Each group has a conception of the way society is
structured, what Hardman calls the model (of the dominant
group) and the counterpart model (the world-structure of the
muted group). ABCD is an unbounded field that represents 'the
wild' or nature, as opposed to 'the social'. This is more relevant to
peripheral groups than to those muted categories that are members
of mainstream society, such as children. As Douglas (1975)
suggests, 'in each constructed world of nature, the contrast between
man and not-man provides an analogy for the contrast between
the member of the human community and the outsider. In the last

inclusive set of categories, nature represents the outsider.' The un-
shaded portion of y is that area of the muted world structure that
is hidden from the dominant group, and the intersection of the
sets represents that part of the muted culture that is revealed to
the dominant group. Thus, the relationship between the area of y
and the intersection of x and y expresses the degree of mutedness,
while the dotted boundary of y suggests that the muted area
merges with the field, it becomes a part of nature.

This model can be used to pin down the internal and external
processes that underlie outsider status. In categorizing gypsies as
an outsider group, for example, we can locate the gypsy world-
structure in the framework of the dominant structure, which gives
us a romantic portion, y minus the intersection, and a deviant
portion, the intersection. The intersection of x and y is an area of
deviance; since that part of gypsy culture that is visible in the
dominant world-structure is detached, it does not appear to be a
part of any culture. Since it does not fit into the social order of
the dominant group, manifestations of gypsy culture are labelled
as deviant. The remainder of the muted set is the world of the
romantic gypsy, who is a part of nature and removed from mainstream society both in space and time. From an urban perspective,
'real' gypsies — that is, those conforming to the romantic myth —
are a rural people; from a rural perspective, 'real' gypsies no
longer exist: they are part of a vanished folk culture. We might
compare Brody's (1975) description of the 'real' Eskimo as con-
ceived by the white community in the Canadian North: 'the
tough, smiling, naive, ultimately irrational soul who, animal-like,
is deeply attracted to roaming the open spaces of the limitless
tundra and ice'. Again, the mythical individual is removed from
the dominant society and merges with nature. There is an interesting similarity between this view of the Inuit and the dominant
society's response to Chicanos in Los Angeles, as described by
Nelson and Clark:

In the decades prior to World War II, migrant farm workers would converge
on Los Angeles each winter. The local newspapers would regularly proclaim
the event a 'Mexican problem' and deplore the relief and hospital load created

by this annual influx ... but during the same period, the area was actively discovering and romanticizing its Spanish heritage. Starting with Helen Hunt Jackson's 'Ramona', a myth was created glorifying an imaginary life of the mission days. ... Further, numerous cities sponsored annual fiesta days, often including a colorful pageant called the ride of the Rancheros Visitadores. [Nelson and Clark, 1976]

The contrast between the manifest deviance of the group and that muted part of the culture that is romanticized clearly reinforces the image of deviance, since to appear to have abandoned a noble existence, in harmony with nature, for one that conflicts with mainstream conceptions of order and harmony is an indication of degeneracy. In the case of gypsies, we could also reverse the labels to demonstrate the dominance of the *gauje* by the gypsy, where the muted part of the settled community is seen in the form of stereotyped images that may be confirmed by encounters with the *gaujes,* particularly in conflict situations. The same principle could be applied to the Inuit and North American Indian conceptions of social structure in relation to mainstream society. The outsiders' view of overlapping world-structures, reversing the positions of dominance and mutedness, is obviously of less consequence than the formulation that puts mainstream society in the dominant role, since it is the latter which has most of the power and which designs policies for control, and these practices are informed by partial and mythical images of outsiders. The minority's view of itself as dominant is important, however, in appreciating its reaction to official policy.

CONCLUSION

In the dominant—muted model, we have a representation of economic and social relationships that has a high level of generality but is capable of elaboration to fit it into specific cultural contexts. The model may converge with a class model of society, for example where ethnic discrimination drives 'those subject to that discrimination into segmented labour markets' (Giddens, 1979),

confirming lumpenproletarian status. However, the muted—
dominant model diverges from the class model, where the muted
or dominated group retains an economic distinctiveness that keeps
it outside the dominant mode of production. To allocate such
groups to the working class without qualification signifies a failure
to recognize that different forms of economic organization and
social structure can function under the umbrella of capitalism.

CHAPTER 3

Models of society and social control

There are a number of institutions in the dominant society that impinge on the economic and social life of outsiders, constraining their activities and modifying their behaviour. Apart from the direct economic relations between peripheral groups and mainstream society, the most important points of contact are with the social control agencies — teachers, social workers, police and local government officers — who, apart from the subversive ones, are all concerned with maintaining the boundaries of the larger society and fitting the peripheral group into its social and economic categories. They implement, at the local level, policies that are informed both by popular attitudes and by central government and which, to a certain extent, they generate themselves. As Pahl recognizes, the relationship between the actors who contribute to the formulation of social control policies is a variable one:

What Poulantzas calls 'the social categories of the state apparatuses' and I call 'the managers of the urban system' will have different styles and ideologies, depending on whether they identify strongly with central authority dominating the periphery or whether, alternatively, they have a degree of autonomy and struggle to support local interests against those of the centre. [Pahl, 1977]

The relationship between the principal contributors to policy in regard to gypsies in England and Wales, for example, would appear to be that the central government has a liberalizing affect on local authorities, which, in turn, may be strongly influenced by popular expressions of antagonism towards travelling people. Variations in practice indicate that differences in goals create tensions that are reflected in shifts between liberality and authoritarianism.

The divergence of interests manifested in policy conflicts, however, masks an essential unity in attitudes to outsiders. These attitudes may reflect subtle differences in political objectives, but to the peripheral group it is their unity that is projected. Popular and official reactions, mediated by the social control agencies, express a model of society that is articulated in varying degrees; and the characteristic responses to outsiders can all be related to this same model, which is essentially the world-structure of the dominant groups in society. As Douglas (1966) suggests, 'people carry round with them a consciousness of social structure. They curb their actions in accordance with the symmetries and hierarchies they see therein, and strive continually to impress their view of the relevant bit of structure on other actors in their scene.' This view of the connection between conceptions of social order and actual interactions is supported by Giddens (1976), who suggests that, in taking up a position in any encounter, people will draw on their social knowledge 'normally in an unforced and routine way'. Conflicts between the larger society and outsider groups are not normal or routine but they do tend to provide a prompt for assertions from hostile communities about the way in which society should be constituted. These declamations from protesters consist essentially of statements about the moral order of society that provide a basis for unfavourable judgements about outsider cultures. This is demonstrated both by local protests and parliamentary debates.

The mainstream social model, which overrides class conflict when the social system is threatened by an outsider group, is necessarily conservative, emphasizing consensus or convergence of interests. The essential elements of the model have a long tradition in social and political philosophy, but the most influential recent advocate of the consensus view is Talcott Parsons, whose systems model is particularly appealing to government agencies concerned with corporate management, where method and efficiency are crucial. Parsons's message is that power in society is the 'capacity of a social system to get things done in its collective interest. This puts an emphasis on an *overriding* collective interest, and upon the *integration* of the system through common values while playing down any discordant interests or internal conflict' (Bottomore, 1975). In other words, as Giddens (1976) argues, conflict of interest can only represent a clash between individual actors and the interests of the collectivity. There are no fundamental *social* cleavages, and there is no place for group conflict as a problematic component of the social structure. Social groups are seen as elements of a system, and in order for the system to be functional the elements must be integrated, in this case by shared values. Of particular interest in the present discussion is that this conception of society is expressed not only in government policy, which might be expected to reflect the 'collective interest', but in protests from groups that, from a different perspective, might be considered exploited, alienated or deprived, such as the residents of low-status council estates. What this reflects is, as E. Ardener (1975) recognizes, 'that all world-structures are totalitarian in tendency'; so that, when a deprived group in the dominant society feels threatened by an outsider group, it will appeal to the collective interest in its expressions of antagonism[1] — identification with dominant interests provides security in the face of a threat. A typical sentiment reflecting this position is contained in a letter to the *Walsall Observer* complaining about Irish travellers:

why, in heaven's name, don't the eighty per cent [*sic*] of the members of a foreign republic stay in their own country and live in houses there, like normal people.

DEVIANCY, DEPRIVATION AND SOCIAL POLICY

Deviancy and deprivation are, by definition, relative concepts. The question we need to consider, however, is what the recognition of deviant behaviour, or of less than acceptable levels of material

---

1 Similarly, Marx and Engels (1968) noted that 'each new class is compelled . . . to represent its interests as the common interest of all members of a society . . . it has to represent [its ideas] as the only rational, universally valid ones.'

well-being, is based upon. In other words, in relation to what social model are people judged to be deviant or deprived? We can then consider the relevance of the social model to peripheral ethnic groups and decide whether or not deviancy and deprivation are fitting labels to describe their social behaviour and economic status.

One danger of adopting a relative perspective is that undue emphasis may be given to those who do the categorizing, to the neglect of the groups or individuals who are identified as deviant or deprived (Plummer, 1979). This leaves us with Becker's relativist position, namely that 'social groups create deviance by making the rules whose infraction constitutes deviance and by applying these rules to particular people and labelling them as outsiders' (Plummer, 1979). While it is necessary to examine the values of the labellers, it is also necessary to consider the factors that make some social groups different from the rest, that is, the structural forces that lead to some groups being identified as outsiders. This is what Corrigan (1978) refers to as a relational perspective, whereby deviance and deprivation are seen as 'predicaments created dialectically in the structured relationships of the deviant or deprived individuals to the rest of society'. Certain consequences follow from being defined as deviant and/or deprived, and the popular and official responses to the subject groups may well reinforce behaviour or economic status.

In the particular instance of peripheral groups like gypsies, it is clear that their imputed deviance results from a divergence between their observed behaviour and the norms of the larger society, which is assumed to hang together on the basis of shared values; the Parsonian consensus model establishes the criteria for measuring the deviance of the peripheral group. As I suggested in discussing the mutedness of peripheral groups in the previous chapter, the unitary view of society articulated in Parsons's model fails to admit alternative world-structures to that of the dominant society. The consensus model cannot conceivably provide an appropriate frame of reference for the analysis of peripheral ethnic minorities because it is totalitarian, and the matching of observed behaviour with the categories of the model can be achieved only with considerable distortion.

A further consequence of the attribution of deviancy and deprivation is that it cuts the labelled group off from the rest of society.
These categories are used as if they were crisply defined sets, but it
would be more appropriate to think of deviancy and deprivation
as fuzzy sets, particularly to avoid stereotyping which involves the
characterization of supposedly negative attributes of social groups
in unambiguous terms.[2] If sets are thought of as fuzzy, things can
be allocated to them according to *degrees* of membership. Thus,
murder would be included in the deviant set in most value systems, but the use of a drug like cannabis might or might not be
included, and the boundary of the set can be described as 'fuzzy'
rather than 'sharp' or 'precise'. This fuzziness is clearly due to a
lack of consensus, but the consensus model cannot accommodate
ambiguity and requires that its categories can be clearly defined.

These conceptual problems have particular implications for
practice. Parsons himself was expressedly concerned with the
realization of his model in social life and suggested appropriate
strategies for creating an integrated society. Thus:

The mechanisms of control in such cases (for example, a delinquent gang)
must operate in situations insulated from the pressures of normal sanction
systems ... a special process of conditional sanctioning of behaviour can
operate until a pattern consistent with the general institutional expectations
is so strongly established that the special permissiveness and support are un-
necessary. [Parsons, 1961]

Control strategies for groups like the Inuit or British gypsies are
less devious than this but are prompted by the same assumption;
that group behaviour should conform with institutional expectations.

At first sight, it might appear that deviancy, but not deprivation, would be a characteristic of a social group requiring corrective action. As commonly applied, the labels 'deviant' and 'deprived'
are opposed. Thus, deviancy can be defined as norm infraction
(the violation of widely accepted standards of behaviour), a negative attribute that needs to be rectified; deprivation suggests a lack

---

2 There is a simple and relevant account of fuzzy set theory by Pierce
(1977).

of material or cultural resources and, in policy terms, implies a positive response, a need to channel resources to the group or individual in order to reduce inequalities. In practice, however, the categories are blurred. The connection that is made between the two is that deprivation is due to social inadequacy — fecklessness, boozing and so on — so an inability to cope with the normal routine of social life can be attributed to deviant behaviour. In fact, when applied to outsider groups like gypsies, both deviancy and deprivation may be recognized as imputed characteristics that legitimate the dominant society's social control policies.

The problem can be brought to ground by describing two cases, both of which have a bearing on social policy. Means (1977), discussing the working of family advice centres in Birmingham, refers to a family in council accommodation who failed to inform the council that their lavatory had broken and they were using their front room for defecation. This behaviour might be interpreted as deviancy, or as an indication of their exploitation or deprivation. Their actions may have been determined by the fact that the family felt alienated and unable to communicate with the bureaucracy, but within the local community, shitting in the front room would certainly be seen as a deviant act. This incident might be compared with an event at a planning inquiry, preceding the establishment of a permanent site for travellers in Liverpool, when a photograph of a stool, abstracted from its larger environment but evidently out-of-doors, was produced in evidence by an objector (P. Scraton, personal communication). Evidently, the purpose of this visual aid was to demonstrate that gypsies are unclean and deviant; but hidden from the inquiry was the gypsy's code of ritual cleanliness, by which a lavatory inside a trailer is considered *mochadi.* In these two cases, the explanation of the 'deviant' behaviour differs, but the official responses would probably be identical.

To argue against mainstream definitions of deprivation is more difficult since peripheral groups may well be deprived in the sense that their traditional resource base has been eroded as a result of the expansion of the dominant economic system, and access to alternative wealth-creating activities is not secured. None the less, officially defined deprivation often reflects ethnocentric bias and would not be considered deprivation in the context of the outsider's world-structure.[3] Travelling people, in particular, as the most conspicuous but at the same time the most muted outsider group in Britain, are frequently referred to as 'deprived'. This is illustrated by a government report on gypsies in England and Wales, based on research carried out in 1965 and 1966, that is replete with comments reflecting the standards of mainstream society and judgements on traveller culture that are inevitably misplaced. The following two extracts typify the ethnocentricity of the report:

Despite the acquisition of some modern amenities, *the travelling life remains inconvenient* and, in many cases uncomfortable, particularly in cold and wet weather, as many daily activities must inevitably take place out-of-doors.

If a caravan is equated with a room, it can be roughly estimated that 65 per cent of traveller families live at a density of more than two persons per room compared with less than 3 per cent of the total population who live at that density. *The position is not quite so serious as these figures suggest* since most caravans can be sub-divided to some extent for sleeping. Although the modern caravan is more spacious than the traditional wagon, it is not necessarily healthier for crowded living since the number of air changes per hour is likely to be less than in the traditional wagon as it is better sealed. [Ministry of Housing and Local Government, 1967]

Having made these unfavourable observations on the travelling life, the report concludes, inevitably, that:

As a result of the increasing affluence of the settled population, the *social* and economic gap between them and the travellers will widen, so that *the task of raising the latter to the general level,* or of giving them the opportunity to reach that level, will become increasingly difficult. [my emphases] [Ministry of Housing and Local Government, 1967]

---

3 Similarly, Basil Bernstein, answering a question about deprivation, argued that 'this notion of treating children as exhibiting various kinds of deficits turns the social scientist into a plumber whose task is to plug, or rather, fill the deficits. It may lead to a partial relation with the child. You see the child as a cognitive or perceptual deficit, and so lose track of the vital nature of the communal experience of the child' Bernstein (1971, postscript). We can compare this with Charlotte Hardman's concept of mutedness. I discuss children as a muted group in chapter 12.

Ethnocentric conceptions of deprivation are similarly evident in recent reports on Irish travellers. Gmelch (1977a), for example, refers to 'the deplorable state of Ireland's itinerant population — the poverty, wretched living conditions, illiteracy, and an infant mortality rate four times that of the settled Irish'. There is an implicit connection between these characteristics of traveller culture which leads one on to the conclusion that they would be better off living in council houses. However, infant mortality might be reduced by providing better access to hospitals and to a supply of clean water, which would not necessarily require travellers to forsake a form of shelter that they find quite adequate and, in many cases, preferable to a house. A similar attitude is evident in a report by Baker and O'Brien (1979), which, in many ways, echoes the English survey 12 years earlier. They describe the living conditions of many travelling families as appalling and see any solution to their problems including provision for tolerable standards of shelter. Specifically, they claim that 'most caravans are clearly inadequate as long-term accommodation, particularly for family households. Space is more restricted than in any but the smallest flat, standards of insulation tend to be much below those of permanent structures so that it is difficult to maintain adequate temperatures in winter, . . .' and so on. However, they do accept that, in exceptional cases, caravans can provide adequate accommodation (meaning, presumably, that they would find them adequate themselves) and that the restrictions on behaviour are less than would be the case if travellers were renting houses in the public or private sector. Admittedly, some work has been done on travelling people in Britain that goes some way to correct this bias, notably research by the Centre for Environmental Studies (Adams *et al.*, 1975[4]), which has had some influence on government policy (Department of the Environment, 1976[5]), but the presumption that gypsies should adopt mainstream standards is a

---

4 Okely's contribution is particularly useful.
5 While acknowledging the work by Adams and others, the author of this report, Sir John Cripps, ignores some of its most important findings and holds to several myths about gypsies. However, some influence is discernable.

persistent one. The significance of this characterization of travellers is essentially functional. Deprivation, like deviancy, is a label derived from the norms of mainstream society, and the object of the categorization is to justify a policy of regulation and constraint. This may be described benignly as acculturation or social assimilation, or as cultural suppression in order to reduce a threat to the dominant system. (For an illustration of this point, see Kearns, 1977.)

The official response to outsiders at the national level is not based on research findings, which probably have no more than a marginal influence on policy, but it does reflect local political pressures to a considerable extent. In this connection, the persistence of the myth of deviancy, and less commonly the myth of deprivation, are important, since they provide continuing justification for a policy of control, that is, one that is intolerant of perceived behaviour. Cohen (1973) has identified the problem of 'deviancy amplification', whereby an initial perception of deviance is transmitted by the control culture and in the process of filtering the information — in the media, for example — stereotypes are created and exploited. This leads to a reaction, with increased deviance, polarization of attitudes, and confirmation of stereotypes.

Cohen's scheme is of some relevance to the outsider problem, although it is not entirely appropriate in cases where the outsiders are ethnic minorities. First, the initial perception of deviance is due to the conflict in norms between the dominant and muted culture, so the deviance may be described as mythical. The image of deviance is then transmitted, particularly in the local newspapers, and amplified in the process. In Cohen's terms, a 'moral panic' ensues, one of which is described in chapter 10. Stereotyping does not lead to increased deviance, however, because the outsider group would not recognize itself as deviant. In fact, some panics prompted by 'invasions' of travellers in Britain hardly involve the travellers at all apart from encounters with local government officers serving eviction notices. As a result of the amplification of mythical deviancy, however, an antagonistic community may be more inclined to distance itself from the outsider group, and there may be a political reaction which results in greater physical and social isolation of the minority, as is evident in many conflicts between travellers and the settled community in British cities. The boundary between the outsiders and mainstream society is thus reinforced, and this contributes to the persistence of the myth of deviancy. Cohen's model is possibly more applicable to groups like native North Americans than to gypsies, since the former, through incorporation into the dominant system, have become dependent. Problems of deviant behaviour, such as alcoholism, may in part be symptoms of dependency, and the reaction of the dominant culture to deviant behaviour in the minority — increased discrimination based on the apparent confirmation of stereotypes — may lead to an increase in deviant behaviour. Again, however, the importance of the element of myth in relation to the perceived deviance of a muted culture must be recognized.

The problems encountered by peripheral groups in their relations with the larger society stem from the inclusive and unitary view of social structure held by those dominant groups that are responsible for managing outsiders with the support of a large cast of people who feel able to subscribe to a consensus view of society. The devaluation of minority cultures and the attempts to integrate them into the dominant society can be understood in these terms. This social model should itself be seen in the context of capitalist economies and those socialist economic systems that were described in the last chapter as expansionary, progressive, and unfolding in a predetermined pattern. Groups within such societies that take a different view of development, or do not see the necessity of development, present a threat to the stability of the system and are, therefore, obvious targets for regulation.

CHAPTER 4

Order and control

In discussing the consensus model, I have suggested that a concern for social order is a necessary consequence of holding to the illusion of a consensus and that, when official policy towards peripheral groups is based on this illusion, they are labelled, inevitably, as deviant or deprived. We need now to consider the concept of order in greater detail and to identify ways by which order is transmitted in the social structure and in the built environment. My interest in this question was prompted by the sorts of prescriptions the central government was making for sites for gypsies in England and Wales following the 1968 Caravan Sites Act (Part II), which requires local authorities to provide permanent sites for travellers. The layout for a model site (figure 2), proposed in a report by a Joint Working Party of the Local Authority Associations and the Gypsy Council (*Caravan Sites Act, 1968, Part II* [n.d.]) clearly puts a strong emphasis on spatial order, and this solution to the settlement problem has been repeated in so many instances that it might be taken as the stock response of authority to non-conforming minorities. Thus, it is necessary to appreciate the appeal of Cartesian geometry in environmental designs for peripheral or non-conforming groups. What are the beliefs that the 'straighteners', as Buttimer (1979) calls them, translate into concrete spatial forms? The significance of this particular site design, and, similarly, government housing for the Inuit or the Australian Aboriginal population, is that it conflicts with the spatial arrangements that the client community creates for itself. The way in which travellers organize their social and economic space is judged

31

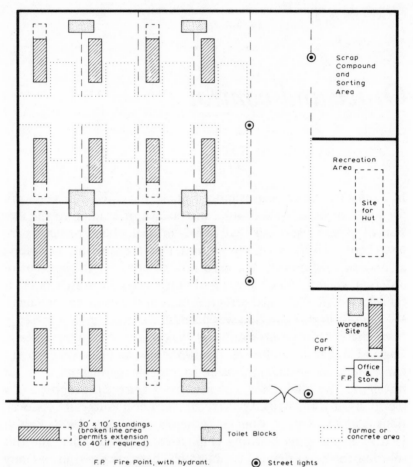

Figure 2 A design for a gypsy trailer site.
(*Source:* Caravan Sites Act, 1968, Part II)

to be deviant by the dominant society, and permanent sites pro-
vded by the government are a device for the correction of deviance.
Before examining this particular problem in greater detail, however, it might be helpful to consider in more general terms the
ideological basis of a concern for social and spatial order.

Disorder is considered to be undesirable in many social contexts, but there is no consensus about the desirability of order
because the attainment or imposition of order invariably puts con-

straints on behaviour, which may be resented. With the possible exception of some Utopian social experiments, the attainment of order requires domination and results in conflict. In the home, for example, keeping the place tidy involves putting constraints on children's play. The parents' preference for order involves domination of the children, although this form of social control seems to the parents to be permissible since it serves an educative function. Socialization within the family into a belief in the absolute value of order is encouraged by the capitalist economic system, demonstrated, for example, by the advertising of dining room suites and fitted kitchens that are designed to create purified domestic environments. Under the capitalist mode of production, there is a strong link between order and material accumulation. At a different scale, the same problem is manifested in the designation of green belts and associated measures to limit the spatial extent of urban areas. The seemingly innocent concern with clear and unambiguous boundaries between city and countryside has important economic consequences, differentially benefiting social classes. Thus, property values in proximity to green belts increase while the restriction on the use of land for residential development increases the scarcity of housing for low-income groups. In stressing the enhancement of amenity that results from greater order in the landscape, the element of class conflict is usually hidden. In this respect, Hardin's (1968) paper, 'The tragedy of the commons', is exceptional, since he argues that wilderness areas would be destroyed if accessible to all so only those 'fit' to appreciate wilderness should have the opportunity to enjoy it. There is in this sentiment a clear connection between amenity and order, the need for control, exclusion and domination. Historically, a similar conflict can be discerned in the eighteenth-century enclosures. The new, ordered, agricultural landscape, described by Barrell (1972) as 'a complete realization of all those attitudes to land . . . characteristic of the rural professional class', was for John Clare alienating and repressive, and his poetry expresses his feeling of loss for the aesthetic disorder of the pre-enclosure landscape. At the root of Clare's protest was what he saw as the increasing domination of the peasantry by the bourgeoisie under the new farming system.

The generality of the problem of order, of form and formlessness, has been recognized by Mary Douglas (1966). She suggests that, 'though we seek to create order, we do not simply condemn disorder. We recognize that it is destructive to existing patterns; also, that it has potentiality. It symbolizes both danger and power.' It is the threatening nature of disorder that is crucial. Parental authority may be undermined if the creative disorder of children's play is allowed to disrupt adult schemes for domestic order; or the working class may threaten middle-class environmental interests. It follows that in the imposition of order it is essential to define boundaries between incompatible categories, whether these are social classes, divisions of space in the home, or categories of land use. As Douglas puts it succinctly, 'Danger lies in marginal states.' This is illustrated by the desire of planners to complete the landscape, to eliminate areas that do not have a clearly defined role in terms of the perceived interests of mainstream society. Davidson (1976), for example, refers to the urban fringe as 'a neglected planning environment. Its opportunities have not been realized; its problems, if they are identified at all, are seen in isolation, neither linked outwards to the activities and resources of the countryside, nor inwards to the demands and needs of the town.' Marginal land is not easily bounded, and if uses are not designated it is difficult to control. Planners evidently feel uncomfortable about land that has no clear functional identity. Boundaries have to be defined, and boundary maintenance involves the imposition of sanctions on those who transgress the boundaries, or the erection of barriers to prevent transgression (what Mary Douglas terms 'pollution'). At the city scale, this is a service provided by the institutional 'gatekeepers', whose concern is to homogenize social and economic space. Mixed uses may be seen as detrimental to amenity and to property values by local authority planners and building society managers, respectively.

The emphasis on order in urban planning, which is particularly relevant to the question of society's treatment of peripheral groups, has been recognized by a number of writers although attempted explanations of the problem have not been particularly revealing. Eversley (1973), for example, argues that British planners have traditionally been advocates of order and, for this reason, intolerant, but he recognizes a fear of totalitarianism which makes people tolerant of disorder, although they do not actually prefer it. This is not very helpful. We need to ask: how much disorder is tolerated, and from whom? Is the disorder threatening, or does it simply provide acceptable variety in the built environment, without doing damage to basic economic or social interests, that is, the interests of the dominant groups in society?

Alexander (1966) provided an interesting graphical conception of the problem when he contrasted the complexity of the 'natural' city with the simplicity of the 'artificial' city, by which he meant the complex capitalist city, in which structures and activities have accumulated over a long period of time, as opposed to the totally planned city, which has been built very quickly and has a singular ideological identity. Alexander called the planned city a tree, that is, a hierarchical structure where the constituent subsets (land uses, for example) do not overlap. By contrast, the 'natural' city can be represented as a semi-lattice, where two overlapping sets belong to the collection and the set of elements common to both also belong to the collection. This makes possible far more combinations of activities than is permissible in a tree-like planned city. To give a simple example, which hardly demonstrates the potential of the model for retaining complexity, backyard iron furnaces could be happily accommodated in an industrial/residential set in a semi-lattice but not in a tree, because the latter contains only collections of single-element sets. There are some doubts about the validity of the semi-lattice model in the light of more recent thinking on the subject,[1] but, more fundamentally,

---

1 For a criticism of Alexander's model, see Harary and Rockey (1976). They conclude that 'A real city is such a complex human institution, consisting of interacting social, economic, and physical phenomena, that it will probably continue to defy mathematical categorization.' However, it is still possible that the application of a mathematical language that allows the retention of more of the complexity of urban spatial structures would be worthwhile in order to counteract the simplifying tendencies of the straighteners. For an approach to the development of such a language, see Hillier *et al.* (1976).

Alexander's explanation of the inadequacies of tree-like cities appears superficial. Like Jacobs (1961) earlier, he sees cities planned on the principle of tree graphs as undesirable because they cannot cater for the essential variety of human experience; but he is guilty of naive managerialism in putting the blame for boring cities in which no one wants to live on the planning profession. Similarly, his explanation for the planners' failure to think in anything but simplified terms is an exclusively psychological one — 'it is because designers, limited as they must be by the capacity of the mind to form intuitively accessible structures, cannot achieve the complexity of the semi-lattice in a single mental act'. This may be true, but it is not a complete explanation. It should be remembered, however, that Alexander wrote this before structuralist analysis became fashionable in urban studies. Sennett (1970) makes a similar comment on the city in Western, industrialized societies in making a case for an anarchist society. Again, he explains a predilection for order in psychological terms. His argument is that, in giving up the protection of the family, the adolescent accommodates the complexity of the world outside by collapsing experience into simplified categories, in what Sennett calls a purification process. This adaptation to complexity is then translated into the social structure, particularly through the agency of those purified individuals who enter the managerial professions, and hence, the 'myth of the purified community' gains currency.[2] This is manifested in expressions of common identity and in the repression of deviants, both of which are expressions of 'men's fear of power within themselves'. Sennett takes a broader view of the problem than Alexander in that he does not see the problem solely as a conceptual one for designers, but in emphasizing possible psychological reasons for the simplification of reality, he neglects the economic and political determinants of order which tend to be concealed in the urban planning process.

---

2 Writing in the late 1940s, Margaret Mead accounted for racialist attitudes in terms similar to Sennett: 'In the anti-[minority] group are found those whose need for consistency is very great, who cannot tolerate ambiguities, who have smoothed out their perception of reality into a tight and perfect structure which presents a smooth, extra well-adjusted aspect, but contains the possibility of a psychotic breakdown' (Mead, 1978).

From this discussion, we can derive two propositions that appear to be plausible and empirically testable. First, any social formation will attempt to maintain itself either by excluding threatening individuals or groups, or by transforming them and incorporating them into the social structure in an acculturation process. This is essentially the position taken by Mary Douglas. Second, in the case of industrialized societies under both capitalist and socialist modes of production, the maintenance of the structure by the dominant class will involve the centralization of power, hierarchical organization of institutions and, in the built environment, the segregation of land uses to exclude activities that threaten the processes of production and reproduction. Significantly, it is in these social formations that systems analysis has assumed an important role in the management of industry and in social administration. In his critique of systems theory, Habermas (1976) has suggested that 'social evolution . . . is projected onto the single plane of the expansion of power through the reduction of environmental complexity'. Simple spatial structures that are functionally homogeneous are easier to control from the centre.

To move from the abstract to the concrete, in capitalist states property is of fundamental importance in the maintenance of the class system, and the significance attached to spatial order in the built environment is a reflection of the role of property in securing the dominance of the bourgeoisie. As Parkin (1979) remarks, one of the two main sets of exclusionary devices that the bourgeoisie constructs is concerned with restricting the benefits of property (the other being credentialism, the control over entry to the professions). Property ownership, he suggests, 'is a form of closure designed to prevent general access to the means of production and its fruits', and he goes on to argue that the control of property should be restored to the centre of class analysis because 'it is the most important single form of social closure common to industrial societies'. This is clearly evident in the conflicts between gypsies and the settled community in Britain, where the violation of property in either private or municipal ownership is the most frequent cause of exclusionary actions by local authorities. This is, however, only a particularly dramatic instance of exclusion that is otherwise effected through the routine operations of the housing market.

In relation to the first proposition, that any social system will employ essentially the same devices of exclusion and incorporation in order to maintain itself, it is notable that social movements that explicitly reject the values of the capitalist system evolve similar forms of social organization. Communes, for example, which might be ostensibly anarchist, in practice depend on consensus and order. As Cotgrove (1976) recognizes, 'the distinctive features of utopias are order and control, even (paradoxically) when the value which is desired to maximize is freedom. The objective is to achieve an ordered, controlled, stable system, to achieve values such as peace, individuality, self-fulfilment, the assured enjoyment of an environment.' Douglas herself has described a number of non-capitalist societies where social and economic life is rigidly structured through the medium of ritual taboo, and the case of gypsies in industrialized societies provides another example.

In applying these arguments to the case of peripheral ethnic minorities, and particularly to an analysis of the official response to gypsies in Britain, I would suggest that the problem is not simply one of conflict between order and disorder, as if these were absolute and unambiguous states. Rather, it is a problem of the imposition of order on the peripheral group by the dominant society, because the economic and social life of the former, as it is manifest in the environment, is *perceived* as disorderly and threatening. The internal order of the peripheral group is hidden, but it exists. For example, if space allows, English travellers arrange their trailers in extended family groupings because great importance is attached to physical proximity, while the internal organization of the trailer is regulated by the dominant members of the family. Children passing in front of seated adults in order to leave the trailer are often given the impossible order to 'watch people's faces', that is, not to walk in front of people. Similarly, objects in the trailer like china ornaments and cushions are usually arranged with great care. This concern with social order and the domestic environment, however, does not extend beyond the trailer because, with a tradition of nomadism, people do not feel an attachment to a particular piece of land and so do not feel an urge to put boundaries around it and defend it, although this is a notable tendency on permanent sites. Thus, there is a social and spatial order in gypsy culture that takes different forms to the order that is valued in mainstream society, and the two modes of order are largely incompatible. In an attempt to understand why gypsies are an outsider group, I would attach more weight to the symbolic forms of order in the larger society than to those that characterize the gypsy's social structure, because exclusion and constraint, prompted by threats to the order of the dominant system, are fundamental in any account of their status. Because the dominant society is a capitalist society, however, it should not be assumed that the argument would be inapplicable to a command economy, where the dominant groups are similarly concerned with securing their position by exclusionary strategies.

CHAPTER 5

The transmission of order

Society reproduces itself by transmitting the dominant ideology through a number of channels. The most obvious one, and the one that has been subject to the most extensive analysis, is the educational system, but there are other institutions that are important transmission agents, including the planning system. In fact, people gain their knowledge of the symbolic order of society from their experience of social and economic relationships and from experience such as that gained in the use of the built environment, largely outside the orbit of formal education. In this sense, the transmissions by which society reproduces itself are primarily diffuse, and they are all, by definition, educational. Bourdieu and Passeron (1977) recognize this in distinguishing three forms of educational transmission:

1. diffuse, where pedagogy is a function of all members of a social formation;
2. family education, whereby parents exercise an educational role in bringing up their children;
3. institutionalized education, by those agents 'explicitly mandated for this purpose by an institution directly, or indirectly, exclusively or partially, educative in function'.

These distinctions are somewhat arbitrary ones, but it is clear that most groups of actors in the social formation are included somewhere. In the last chapter, I stressed the importance of the family in socializing individuals into a belief in the virtues of environmental order; the following discussion has particular relevance to institutions such as local planning authorities in Britain.

Planning authorities are important in the British context because they have a direct role in formulating and implementing policies for the settlement of travellers, and we need to identify the ideological basis of their actions. Planners fit into the third of Bourdieu and Passeron's categories, in that they have to sell policies to elected representatives and to the public, through public relations exercises, for example; and apart from this directly educational function, they reinforce beliefs about the social and economic order by promoting and restricting development, a process that we might call indirect institutional education. Bearing in mind that planners are only one group of agents, dependent on other more powerful ones in the social formation, we can legitimately examine their impact on peripheral groups.

In the following discussion, my concern is primarily with concrete expressions of the economic and social order in capitalist states, but the analysis of the processes by which ideology assumes material forms has wider relevance, for example, to an understanding of the organization of institutions. The essential argument has been developed by Basil Bernstein (1971, especially chapter 11) in relation to formal education, although he has considered briefly the implications of his thesis for problems of environmental design and control. After outlining his ideas, I will consider their specific application to planning problems and to the relationship between government and peripheral ethnic minorities.

Bernstein's immediate concerns are language and the organization of the curriculum in schools, but his theory relates more fundamentally to power structures and the principles of control in society. Taking his analysis of the curriculum as a starting point, Bernstein distinguishes between a *collection* curriculum and an *integrated* curriculum. The collection curriculum is characterized by strong boundaries between subjects, with an emphasis on those aspects that differentiate them. An integrated curriculum, by contrast, connects seemingly disparate areas of knowledge and emphasizes *deep structure*, which renders the traditional boundaries between subjects weak or redundant. The difference between the two is in their *classification*, with a strongly classified curriculum having clear, strongly defined boundaries between subjects and a

weakly classified curriculum having weak, or permeable, boundaries. The boundary is crucial, since boundary maintenance
requires authority: 'If the rules of exclusion are strong, the boundaries well-marked, then it follows that there must be strong
boundary maintainers (authority). If things are to be kept apart,
there must be some strong hierarchy to ensure the apartness of
things.' Thus, in the extreme, we may characterize strong classification as authoritarian and weak classification as anarchistic.

Bernstein makes a further distinction between classification,
which concerns the external boundaries of subjects in the curriculum, and *frame*, which refers to the way in which knowledge
within a subject is transmitted. Strong framing signifies that there
is little potential for varying the method of transmission and
weak framing the reverse. The same concepts can be applied to
speech codes, which can be *restricted* or *elaborated*. The restricted
code is a syntax with few choices in the combination of lexical
terms, and is thus equivalent to the collection curriculum; an
elaborated code is one that generates a large number of choices.
Again, classification and framing define the possibilities for variation and elaboration.

As his analysis of the curriculum demonstrates, Bernstein's
model has important political implications. Strong classification
requires a hierarchical structure for the transmission of authority,
with communication occurring vertically within subjects but hori-
zontally between subjects only at the top of the hierarchy because
of the strength of inter-subject boundaries. Since authority rests
on the maintenance of strong boundaries, any attempt to blur
identities and mix categories threatens the structure and will be
resisted. Following Mary Douglas, Bernstein suggests that 'any
attempt to weaken or change classification strength (or even frame
strength) may be felt as a threat to one's identity and may be experienced as pollution endangering the sacred'. More generally,
Douglas (1966) has argued that the identification of polluting
categories is a means of protecting a social system from challenge.[1]

---

1 Peter Taylor (1976) makes a similar point about conformist tendencies in
   institutions in discussing the organization of geography in British universi-
   ties.

This suggests that a curriculum, or a social formation, that was structured in an integrated fashion, with weak classification and framing, would be more diverse and more tolerant. Deviance, for example, would be less visible because the mixing of categories is permissible. Douglas (1966) makes this point in suggesting that an individual who was mentally ill would be tolerated within the community but, once that person had entered a mental hospital — an institution characteristic of a strongly classified social system — tolerance would be withdrawn because admission to the hospital involves crossing a boundary and entering an excluded category. Conversely, she suggests that, if the mentally ill were accommodated in the community, implying weak classification, they would not be labelled as deviant or different and in need of isolation. Fincher (1978) notes that mental patients taken out of institutions in the United States are not easily accepted into the community by normal residents. This she attributes to the fact that they have been categorized as mentally ill in the first place. People feel much more uncomfortable about mental illness if it is diagnosed as such than about the same behaviour if it is not. Thus, she concludes that 'the attribution of inherent difference, or deviance, to the mildly mentally retarded or ill is a socially constructed phenomenon' (obviously); and, citing Scott (1972), she accounts for this social construction in terms of the need of a society to protect its value system against 'perceived threats of chaos and anomaly'. Her analysis is clearly identical to that of Douglas and Bernstein, and they all point to the need for a weakening of classifications.

Bernstein has a major reservation about weak classification and intergrated codes, however. He suggests that, 'while integrated codes at the surface level create weak or blurred boundaries, at the bottom, they may rest upon *closed, explicit ideologies*'. Thus, we have a necessary emphasis on deep structure in the integrated curriculum, unanimity at an ideological level holding together apparently diverse subject matter. This may resolve Cotgrove's paradox, that utopias of anarchist inspiration require order and control and, thus, ideological consensus. This has important implications for the structuring of social space which will be considered below.

We can apply this scheme for the analysis of educational transmissions to an analysis of spatial structures, particularly to those
environments that are concerned explicitly with control. Essentially, control requires the purification of space and the maintenance of unambiguous external boundaries, and Bernstein has
considered the possible application of his model to this particular
design problem in a paper concerned with the coding of objects
and modalities of control (Bernstein, 1975). He illustrates his
argument with the case of lavatory design, where the room can
range from one that has an explicit single function, reflected in the
furniture and decor — simple, pristine and shining white — and
where there are strong rules of exclusion, to one that can be used
for reading or conversation and is not clearly separated from the
rest of the house in functional terms. The principal variation is in
boundary strength, from strong to weak classification, and the
different functional concepts clearly reflect different ideologies in
the family. Bernstein also considers the physical manifestations of
framing. This refers to the possible number of relationships
between objects (or activities) contained within a space, thus retaining the external/internal distinction between classification and
frame used in analysing the curriculum content and pedagogy,
respectively. However, a potentially large number of relationships
between objects in a space is a function of weak classification of
those objects, so framing could be described equally as classification, the only difference being one of scale. The dustbin screen in
figure 3, for example, suggests an obsessively strong classification
of an object within a yard or garden, and we might guess that this
larger space will also be strongly classified.

Apart from these domestic examples, which are important in
the socialization process at the family level, we can consider the
process of classification in the allocation of space at the urban
level, and particularly the classification manifested in the state's
management of land, which has a direct bearing on the fortunes of
peripheral minorities. In general, the state's activities are directed
to the reproduction of the social formation, which in capitalist
states includes the reproduction of productive capital and the
reproduction of the labour force. As it affects spatial structure,

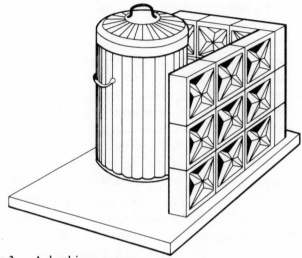

Figure 3   A dustbin screen.
(*Source:* Beadle, D., 1976)

this means that the state has a strong interest in order. Manufacturing processes, for example, can generally be carried on most
efficiently (that is, in terms of the firm's profitability) on land
that is assembled in large parcels and serviced to meet the needs of
particular industries. The segregation of uses that this entails, however, results in greater journey-to-work costs than if industry were
integrated with housing, but trends towards greater segregation of
industry are encouraged by the state through single-use zoning —
that is, strong classification — and space is purified by the exclusion or elimination of non-conforming uses. In the residential
sector, the development of socially homogeneous estates by the
local authority, and the encouragement of homogeneity elsewhere,
for example through development control policy (and supported
by building society mortgage allocation policies), reinforces
boundaries between social groups and gives people a stake in a
particular territory, encouraging conservatism. Thus, Sennett's
'purified community' might be described alternatively as strongly
classified social space that serves to reproduce a conservative
labour force.

Conflict between house-dwellers and travellers in England and
Wales considered from this perspective suggests that, the greater
the social and economic homogeneity of the residential area, the
more visible is the external threat, or pollution, and the greater the
antagonism towards the outsiders. In fact, the position of gypsies
in Britain, viewed historically, appears to confirm the importance
of increasing classification in the management of the urban economy by the local state in relation to the identification of travellers
as outsiders. As a 'problem', there is evidence that they have
become more conspicuous as spatial order in housing and industry
has increased. However, we might question whether the increasing
spatial segregation of social groups is invariably the result of state
action in support of the dominant class. Against this argument, we
might consider the contradiction between the Greater London
Council's policy of racially integrated local authority housing and
the preference of Bengalis, in the face of external threats, to have
segregated housing.[2] Particularly in relation to ethnic minorities,
it is important to note the distinction between external boundaries
defined and maintained by the state, and those boundaries that are
internal in origin, defined by ethnic groups themselves.

Bernstein's ideas on coding and classification could have general
relevance to the analysis of problems of domination and control.
In the organization of institutions and in the built environment,
we can identify varying strengths of classification and framing,
manifested in the form of collections and structures that show
varying degrees of integration. In political terms, these forms can
be associated with, on one hand, centralized, hierarchical systems
and, on the other, autonomous or anarchistic communities. In
relation to peripheral groups, this model is useful for understanding external constraints, the design of institutional environments,
internal expressions of order, and the conflict between outsiders
and mainstream society.

---

2 This is a local issue in the Borough of Tower Hamlets, in the east end of
London, where there is a concentration of Bengalis: the National Front is
active, and the ethnic minority is not confident that it will receive adequate protection from the police.

CHAPTER 6

Outsiders – a résumé

At this point, it might be useful to try and locate peripheral groups in relation to other social groups, using a framework that combines the contributions of the social structure of the minority itself and of the constraints imposed by the larger society in the creation of outsider status. It is possible to do this only in an approximate and schematic way because of variations in the constitution of both peripheral groups and the larger societies of which they are on the margins, which gives rise to a number of possible relationships.

One approach to this problem has been developed by Mary Douglas (1973). In an attempt to characterize small social groups imbedded in larger social structures, and at the same time to relate individuals to societies in terms of the degree of membership or involvement, she has suggested an analytical framework based on two dimensions. These she calls 'grid', referring to the system of classifications used by a society for the communication of ideas, and 'group', a shorthand for inter- and intra-group relationships. Less mysteriously, we could call these axes of participation and domination, respectively (figure 4). On the participation axis, we have at one pole social groups that enjoy a shared classification system — categories are mutually understood and so there is a high level of communication between individuals; it is not always necessary to be expliicit to be understood. In Bernstein's terms, this is a situation where a restricted code is adequate for communication because common experience creates shared meanings. There is no need for a higher level, universal or elaborated code that will

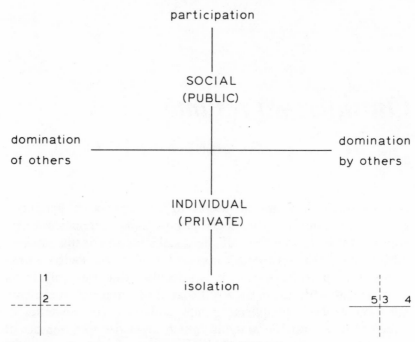

Figure 4   Outsider groups and the larger society.

transcend differences between groups within a larger social system. At the other pole, is the individual who has a private classification system and is thus unable to communicate, but, moving towards the horizontal axis, we can locate individuals who are non-conformists, who can communicate with others in the social structure, and who are able to challenge socially accepted classifications. One basic division on the participation axis is between the upper, public, or social segment and the lower, private, or individual segment. On the horizontal, domination, axis, there is a range from dictatorship, from the extreme left, where an individual has the power to dominate the rest of society, to the situation on the right, where an individual or a small group is dominated by others.

This scheme can be readily adapted to accommodate peripheral groups. Since we are concerned with social groups, the lower, private half of the diagram can be ignored while few peripheral societies would get into the upper left quadrant because their capacity to dominate others is very limited. Within the upper right quadrant, however, outsider groups could occupy a number of alternative locations. Since groups like gypsies and the Inuit are closely integrated communities, have a high level of shared meanings and communicate entirely in a restricted code, they can be placed high up on the participation axis (1). However, if we define them on this dimension in relation to the dominant society, they appear as muted groups and could be placed close to the horizontal axis because their classification systems have little in common with those of the larger society (2). We might note that social policy is generally designed to pull peripheral groups higher up on the participation axis, particularly through formal education that is concerned with the transmission of mainstream values. On the domination axis, there are again different possibilities. Some outsiders, like gypsies in the United States, demonstrate a high level of autonomy (3); others, like some native North American communities, are highly dependent (4), and, finally, we have the possibility of a group crossing the vertical axis and assuming a dominant role in relation to the larger society (5). In some instances, gypsies might occupy this position. It is often argued that increasing dependency is characteristic of peripheral groups in capitalist societies, but there is also evidence that some minorities have the capacity to resist incursions by the state and capital and so retain their autonomy to some degree. It is in any case reasonable to assume that the location of peripheral groups on this axis will shift according to changes in the economy of the dominant system and changes in the governmental response to outsiders. In order to give these generalizations some substance, however, it will be necessary to look at the historical experience of peripheral groups in different national contexts.

CHAPTER 7

The traveller economy

An account of the way in which gypsy communities have adapted to the dominant society, and, more specifically, have been accommodated in the urban spatial structure, requires two perspectives. Clearly, it is necessary to explore the points of contact between traveller society and mainstream society, where stereotypes are formed and official policy originates. Thus, the area of overlap between the dominant and minority world-structures defines the problem from one point of view. However, while it is obvious that official and popular perceptions and the state's response are based only on that part of gypsy culture that is revealed to the dominant society, if we are to assess the impact of external constraints, a description of traveller culture in its own right is also required. This must be a starting point in an assessment of the larger society's impact on the gypsy community's economic and social networks. Thus, to provide a foundation for a critical analysis of policy, the emphasis of this chapter will be on the gypsy's use of the *gauje* world, as if mainstream society were 'out there', beyond the boundary of the traveller community, presenting opportunities for exploitation. While this bias will need to be corrected later, it should provide a counter to the more commonly advanced argument, namely that travellers are being incorporated into the dominant system or are experiencing a modernization process and that changes are induced by the larger society. This view suggests that gypsies do not have the capacity to adapt to economic and political changes of external origin and that their status is determined entirely by forces beyond their control. It is difficult for a *gauje* to interpret the gypsy's world-view, but it is desirable to make an attempt in order to get close to the gypsy community's view of mainstream society.

Even within Western, industrialized societies, it would be imprudent to generalize about the way in which gypsies have adapted to the dominant system because, as Kornblum and Lichter (1972) observe, contrasting urban environments demand different adaptive strategies. More specifically, we could argue that variations in strategies for the management of cities, in the interplay of business and industrial interests and the technocracy, condition the gypsy community's accommodations to the larger society. Thus, it may be more realistic to portray the gypsy economy as it has developed in, say, Los Angeles, as if it represented one-way exploitation of the dominant system, than it would be to portray it as it has developed in London or Paris, where government regulation is an important consideration. A further difficulty results from the fact that the official response to travelling people, which is generally thought of as limiting their freedom of action, may at the same time create new economic opportunities, for example through the provision of welfare benefits. This possibility makes it unrealistic to exclude a consideration of government policies entirely in discussing the workings of the gypsy economy, but for convenience the official response is given a fuller treatment in subsequent chapters. Most of the following discussions refers to travellers in the United Kingdom and the Republic of Ireland, with brief asides on gypsy communities in North America and some European countries, and the limitations of this parochial view should be recognized. My observations largely confirm the findings of Acton (1974) and Okely (Adams *et al.*, 1975), which means that there is little new in this analysis, beyond a particular focus on urban adaptations;[1] but the discussion should serve to demonstrate the connection between the traveller economy and spatial behaviour.

---

1 See also Okely (1976).

OFFICIAL STATISTICS

Economic analyses usually include hard facts, and as a preface to
this account of the gypsy economy it is worth noting the official
attempts that have been made to collect statistics on British
travellers and to consider their political implications. The two
principal data sources are a 1967 report, *Gypsies and other Travellers,* dealing with England and Wales, and *Scotland's Travelling
People,* produced by Gentleman and Swift for the Scottish
Development Department in 1969. In discussing economic activity
at the national level, one would normally utilize official statistics,
but the information contained in these reports is highly suspect.

The 1967 report was designed to provide data on population
distribution, economic activities and social organization that
could provide a basis for policy formulation. The collection of
information, however, was left to local authority representatives,
and the authors of the report admit that councils responded with
varying degrees of efficiency and enthusiasm. This is reflected in
the population statistics, which were collected in March, before
any migrations for agricultural work would have started so that
urban concentrations would have been at a maximum. There is a
strong suspicion of undercounting, particularly in urban areas.
Leeds, for example, had 21 families and Hull none. Eight years
later, according to an estimate made by the Gypsy Council, there
were about 100 families in Leeds and, according to my own estimate, there were at least 60 families in Hull who had a long
association with the city. While numbers do fluctuate owing to
migrations, increases of this order over an eight-year period seem
improbable. The importance of this is not so much that the survey
was inaccurate but that the statistics were accepted by the central
government as correct and included in an appendix to a government circular, 26/66, as an estimate of the demand for sites. As
the provision of sites for travellers is a highly contentious issue,
local authorities were clearly tempted to make a low return in
order to minimize their obligation. Beyond this, statistics that, on
the admission of the authors, were of questionable value were
translated into a map and a table of 'the density of the traveller

population (a) per 1,000 total population and (b) per 1,000 acres in each county and county borough', while another table purported to show the age distribution of travellers.

Thus, through manipulation, data of dubious reliability assumed the status of facts. The central government eventually conceded that the 1967 survey was virtually useless, and in 1978, the Department of the Environment initiated a series of twice-yearly counts of caravans, to be made by local authority officers. This could give only a crude estimate of the size of the population, since there is considerable variation in the number of people per trailer and many families now have two trailers. Again, however, there has been some suspicion that returns have been falsified. Speaking in a House of Lords debate on the Caravan Sites Bill in 1979, Lord Avebury referred to some authorities that refused to participate in the first count and others that gave inflated totals of the number of trailers on permanent sites in order to show that they had fulfilled their obligation under the 1968 Caravan Sites Act (House of Lords, 1979, 1064–5). The London Borough of Bromley, for instance, indicated that it had 51 trailers on authorized sites, but according to Lord Avebury the correct figure was 21. He spoke of 'skilful evasion' by local authorities as a principal reason for the failure of the legislation. I will discuss the political implications of official attempts to collect information on travellers in an account of state–gypsy relations in chapter 9, but I would suggest here that the distortion of statistics for political purposes is a general one and the surveys of travellers are not exceptional in this respect. Miles and Irvine (1979) maintain that, occasionally, 'official statistics are . . . manipulated in attempts to adjust the terms of a political debate', and generally, the concepts employed in the production of statistics serve the purposes of the dominant groups in society. Thus, social statistics should be subject to critical examination in a political context.

A more fundamental problem, demonstrating the difference between the world-structures of the dominant society and travelling people, is the tendency to place travellers in mainstream occupational categories. This was a notable feature of both *Gypsies and other Travellers* and the Scottish Development Department report. In both surveys, men and women were asked their occupations but only a single answer was admissible. Thus, in the English survey agriculture was distinguished from dealing, that is, all types of trading, notwithstanding the fact that farmwork is an occasional occupation, usually harvesting, and is viewed by travellers as a supplement to the income derived from dealing and other activities. More remarkable is the distinction between 'hawker' and 'housewife', as if these were exclusive categories. Although women do most of the housekeeping in traveller families, they may also do scrap work or driving, and in most families the mother would be expected to go 'calling' (hawking). In fact, she may consider the latter as an occupation that provides the greatest satisfaction, since selling to the *gaujes* requires particular skills and this role confers an independent economic status on a woman (Okely, 1975). At the same time, in response to a question from a *gauje* interviewer, a woman may prefer to represent herself as a housewife, recognizing the interviewer's expectations and possibly wishing to conceal her calling role, particularly if allowed only one answer. Thus, while hawking is a common occupation, its importance is unlikely to be reflected in statistics. The inappropriateness of the occupational classification used in the surveys accounts for the very low figure of 8 per cent of women in England and Wales and 4 per cent in the Scottish survey (in winter) who gave their occupation as hawker. The impossibility of fitting travellers into single job categories was not appreciated in these reports, but this was an unconscious ethnocentric bias.[2]

It could be objected that recent research has demonstrated the methodological inadequacy of these early surveys and that official policy is now informed by analysis that is more sympathetic to traveller culture. However, we still find in government documents, notably the Cripps report (Department of the Environment,

---

2 There was also a failure to appreciate the traveller's attitude to the institutions of the dominant society. This is evident in *Gypsies and Other Travellers*, where there is a remarkably naive admission that 'counties and county boroughs were advised to consider the use of local police officers where possible to carry out the survey since experience has shown that they had most knowledge of the whereabouts of travelling people', and, in fact, 47 per cent of the questionnaires were administered by police officers.

1976), a tendency to characterize traveller culture and to formulate policy in terms of discrete and exclusive categories, particularly in regard to work and land use, and this conception could lead to a transformation of traveller culture if strong controls were exercised by the state. This tendency is clearly symptomatic of the general categorization problem in positive social science. The relations of the phenomena that give them meaning, that is, the relations that give things significance in a particular cultural context, are lost in the attempt to generalize and to provide neutral classifications. In abstracting facts from their cultural context, the general appropriateness of categories that are culturally specific is wrongly assumed.[3] In the case of the gypsy economy, the significance of an activity can be appreciated only if it is seen in relation to other activities in the economic system and in relation to the social structure. In turn, the pattern of work in the gypsy economy has to be seen as a response to opportunities created by the mainstream economy. Thus, economic functions are intelligible only if seen in the broader context of gypsy culture and all forms of relationship between the gypsy community and the dominant society.

ECONOMIC ADAPTATIONS TO MAINSTREAM SOCIETY

The essence of the traveller economy has been identified by Okely (Adams *et al.*, 1975) as involving the supply of goods and services where there are gaps in the market in time or space and where any

---

3 As Gregory (1978) notes, in reviewing Bachelard's discussion of the dialectic between phenomenon and relation, categorization can involve the 'tearing apart of the interpenetrating webs' that suspend phenomena in a particular cultural context. Gunnar Olsson (1974) has suggested, significantly, that this view of the world is connected with the functions of the state in centralized political systems. Thus: 'If the human condition actually is a groping kind of activity, characterized by the perpetual struggle between ambiguity and certainty, then an analytical approach which initially assumes all ambiguity away must produce a false picture; one half of reality will be overexposed while the other will be left in darkness. The result is distorted theory and inhibited practice, well reflected in the thingification and dehumanization produced by centralized bureaucracy.'

large-scale or permanently established business would be un-economic or insecure. Thus, travellers can use their mobility and small scale of operation to advantage in exploiting the dominant system. Perhaps more fundamental, however, is the gypsy's view of the *gauje* world as presenting changing opportunities for economic gain so that a premium is put on adaptability. As one traveller has often remarked to me, 'They can turn their hand to anything.' As Acton (1974) has argued, 'superior flexibility in the pursuit of profit is itself referred to as a justifiable source of ethnic pride. This can almost institutionalize change, and removes from it the pain of newness; disregarding tradition is itself a tradition, in certain circumstances.' He goes on to suggest that this ability to adapt brings the traveller closer to the neoclassical economic model of rational economizing behaviour than most other groups. This assertion may have some basis of truth, but it requires considerable qualification in view of the external constraints on economic activity. Adaptability, however, is generally characteristic. Most activities that travellers engage in are also modes of employment that are recognized in the larger society; but, whereas the *gauje* will tend to occupy the same economic role for life, travellers try to find new economic niches as the economy of the settled society changes. This may or may not require spatial mobility, but, more importantly, the traveller acquires skills that allow him to enter into economic relationships with *gaujes* on his own terms, to maintain a dominant role in transactions. To the traveller, the settled community appears passive and exploitable.

In describing the economy of British travellers, I will consider production and consumption, both of which are misinterpreted by the dominant society. Productive activity is maligned while consumption patterns are assumed to indicate deprivation or, less commonly, unseemly affluence. Manifestations of economic life contribute to the negative stereotype, and this is important because the official response is conditioned by the mythology.

Production

It will be useful to catalogue the characteristic occupations of travellers in order to indicate the gaps in the mainstream economy that they have tended to fill, and this, in turn, will go some way to explaining their spatial distribution within urban areas. In compiling a catalogue, however, it is essential to bear in mind the role of work in the gypsy community, discussed above. Two points may be emphasized. First, some activities are carried on only periodically while some occupations may be followed simultaneously. Second, travellers, by retaining a certain degree of autonomy, have not been affected by the separations that constrain work opportunities in the mainstream capitalist system – between occupations, between formal education and work, between workplace and home and, to a lesser extent, between the economic roles of men and women. We might add that there is no separation in the social structure between old people, children and the rest of the community, and, in their cosmology, between life and death.[4] In general, work should be discussed within the context of an integrated social and economic life. In this account, I will follow Okely's classification of gypsy occupations whereby activities are grouped into three categories: services, sale of goods, and seasonal labour. These are not exclusive categories. A service like the clearance of domestic rubbish, for example, may yield saleable materials, but, given a certain arbitrariness, they do represent distinct emphases in employment.

Scrap metal dealing. The scrap component of the raw material input to the British steel industry is about 50 per cent, and most of this is collected by large firms. There is, however, a considerable amount of scrap metal that is generated in small quantities and in dispersed locations, such as domestic scrap, abandoned cars, and

---

4 Okely (1979) asserts that 'Death is equivalent to assimilation' ... 'The place of death (the Gorgio hospital) and the burial place (the Gorgio graveyard) are significant in Gypsy identity but not as symbols of continuity. The individual dead person is dispatched from the living and from the Gypsy group.' This is contrary to my own observation, which is that the dead are referred to in the present tense for years after death, photographs of the dead are valued and occasionally displayed in the trailer, and the birthday of the dead person is remembered, again, as if he were alive. Graveyards do appear to be important symbols of continuity since they are visited frequently.

that produced by small firms in the metal industries. There are also occasional supplies of scrap from industries that are discarding plant but are not regular sources of scrap materials — British Rail, for example. When supplies fluctuate or are not concentrated in large quantities, it is often uneconomical for large firms to collect, but travellers can take advantage of their mobility and of the fact that they may not be entirely dependent on scrap metal dealing for their income, to collect and sort small lots of scrap that may, in total, constitute a considerable proportion of the scrap supply to manufacturing industry.

This is a prime example of filling in gaps in the market in time or space. Statistics on the travellers' contribution to the scrap supply are suspect, being based on estimates made by large dealers to whom travellers make deliveries. Okely (Adams *et al.*, 1975), and later Cripps (Department of the Environment, 1976), cite the 20 per cent figure given in a 1968 report on the industry by the Civic Trust; Gmelch (1977b) got an estimate of 50 per cent from metal dealers in the Dublin area; and Cripps reports a figure of 80 per cent for one local authority in the West Midlands. Although we must accept that these figures may be only rough approximations, travellers evidently have an important role in scrap supply in some industrial areas. Beyond the value of the metal supplied to industry, as Gmelch notes, they also remove abandoned cars and appliances from roadsides, saving local authorities the cost of clearance. However, Okely (1976) suggests that the gypsies' contribution is 'ideologically dispensable', in that 'there is a subtle shift in status as the production of iron and steel moves from a maligned scavenging activity (the gypsies' work) to that of manufacturing'. This is illustrated by the comment of a local authority planning officer, who maintained that gypsies follow 'obnoxious trades, particularly metal dealing' (*Public Health Inspector*, 1968). With a growing awareness of resource scarcity and a consciousness of ecological problems in industrialized societies, evident in some local authority experiments in the recycling of waste products, it is ironic that travellers' activities in this field are condemned. There is ample evidence from local protests that scrap dealing by gypsies contributes to an image of deviancy. In particular, the pro-

cessing of scrap on unofficial stopping places, involving the separation of metals and the burning off of the non-metallic parts of
motor vehicles, contributes to a negative stereotype. This work is
considered 'polluting', primarily because it is done at home and
does not fit into the accepted land use categories of the dominant
society. It is notable that the allocation of space on official sites
generally conforms to the categorical principles employed in land
use planning in Britain, which makes scrap sorting an unacceptable
activity on sites, notwithstanding the economic benefits derived
from it.

Most travelling families in Britain do some scrap work. In
Okely's sample of 111 families, 93 per cent of men said they did
some scrap and it was a major occupation for 65 per cent; 51 per
cent of women did scrap and for 9 per cent it was a major activity.
The role of women in scrap metal dealing is an interesting feature
of travellers' work in that it indicates the importance of the family
as an economic unit. Children are also regularly involved in scrap
sorting, and this is as important educationally as it is economically.
In relation to the woman's contribution, however, it is notable
that men do not reciprocate by engaging in domestic work —
women are discriminated against both within the traveller community and in the larger society.

There is considerable variation in the scale of operation and in
the wealth derived from it. Gentleman and Swift (1971) note that
in Scotland some travellers had regular contracts with factories
generating large quantities of scrap and would sell directly to the
steel mill. Similarly, Okely found families who had contracts with
local authorities for abandoned car disposal. Many families, however, possibly the majority, depend on small irregular supplies and
sell to dealers rather than directly to the consumer, while my own
observations suggest that 'tip-raking' may be as important as collection from other sources for poorer families. Metal collected on
one visit to a refuse tip near a city in the north of England in
1978, for example, was weighed in for £80, that is, the average
industrial wage for about three hours work, although in this case,
two people were involved in collection sorting and delivery. For
travellers who do scrap dealing on a small scale, the work appears

to be occasional, reflecting fluctuations in metal prices and the availability of other sources of income, and is not particularly lucrative. If, however, scrap dealing is to constitute the principal source of income, it is evident that mobility is important and that there must be a considerable investment in capital.

In regard to mobility, Gentleman and Swift (1971) observed that inter-urban variations in metal prices and supplies made 100- to 150-mile round-trips from Glasgow economical, and it is clear that local travellers who restrict their collections to one urban area have fewer opportunities for large profits. Opportunities are also limited by the nature of stopping places and by the hospitality offered by the local authority. Roadside verges may have little space for storage and sorting, while some official sites have none, and evictions by councils make it generally difficult to engage in dealing. Conversely, if a traveller's scrap business becomes highly capitalized, with rented premises, lorries, hoists, cutting equipment and so on, and involves contract work, flexibility is lost — he is in competition with *gauje* dealers, and his operation is more likely to be subject to scrutiny by the local authority. Under the Scrap Metal Dealers Act, 1964, all dealers in England and Wales must register with the local authority and must keep receipts of their transactions. Apart from the difficulty of complying with the law of illiterate, there is clearly an advantage in small-scale and occasional dealing in that it makes it easier to avoid involvement with authority. The small-scale dealer is in a better position to shift to different locations and different occupations as profit margins fluctuate, and can thus minimize dependence on the host society. Increasing the scale of operation may mean abandoning an economic niche.

This question of economic autonomy is also important in relation to official site provision. It is notable that Okely found that, as a major activity, scrap sorting was carried on more frequently on illegal stopping places than on official sites, and that Cripps found it necessary to argue for greater provision for scrap dealing on sites, because it contributes to the national economy and reduces dependence on social security payments (Department of the Environment, 1976). Thus, in official attitudes to scrap work there is a conflict between the desire to regulate travellers as a deviant minority, most evident at the local level, and a desire to secure their economic independence, with the former attitude being the prevalent one.

Other service activities. The collection of waste materials other than scrap metal is organized on a similar basis, in that small quantities are collected from scattered points in an urban area or a larger region. In the past, rag collection has been an important element in the traveller economy, particularly in cities, but low prices have made it uneconomical as a major occupation. In Hull, most rag collection is done by non-gypsy rag-and-bone men (tatters) in combination with scrap collection, using a horse and dray or a pram. This activity is associated exclusively with nineteenth-century working-class residential areas, where there are yards that can be used for sorting materials and wasteland that provides grazing for horses. Gypsies live in close proximity to the tatters and interact with them socially, but their contribution to the trade is now a minor one. Redevelopment of these residential areas is further reducing the scope for this kind of work. Hawking, or calling, provides another opportunity for collecting old clothes, which are used primarily in the traveller's own family. This is one of the incidental benefits of calling, which also serves to inform travellers about possible work opportunities in the neighbourhood, such as small building jobs, tarmacking and gardening (Gmelch, 1977b).

Sale of goods. With some important exceptions, selling is done on a small scale, with minimal outlay on goods and equipment. Calling by women is the commonest form of selling, and the money derived from this can be an important element of the family income, particularly when other work is not available. Since most women do not have access to a car or lorry, calling tends to be restricted to the city, where lack of private transport is not a serious obstacle to door-to-door selling. Women will work an area either singly or in groups, usually from the same extended family. Among travellers in Hull, it is becoming increasingly common for men to drive their wives to small towns up to 50 miles from the city where they can sell without competition from other travellers. This practice tends to be restricted to the more affluent and more mobile families, and it reinforces economic distinctions between families in the same community. There are seasonal variations in calling, with the period before Christmas being a particularly good time for going out with the basket, and it is then that manufactured goods, such as lace, combs and charms, will be complemented by hand-made goods, particularly roses made from toilet rolls and crysanthemums made from dyed elderwood shavings. Hand-made pegs do not have the same seasonal variation.

Although craft goods are still characteristic of the traveller economy, the existence of a craft tradition among travellers lends support to the 'real gypsy' myth, through association with a rural past. Implicit in the dominant society's admiration of a craft industry among travellers is the notion that other occupations, such as the sale of manufactured goods, are parasitic and, by association, that those travellers who do not appear to make goods by hand are also parasitic. Like scrap dealing, the activity is devalued and contributes to a negative image. There is clearly a market for manufactured goods, however, and a woman will exploit it by projecting a 'gypsy' image, that is, by conforming to a stereotype: 'By eliciting the pity of the *gauje* she can extract a greater economic return (Okely, 1975).

The essentially local nature of calling contrasts with selling by travellers on a regional or national basis. Particularly notable in this regard is the growth of antique dealing, which requires a large investment in vehicles for transporting furniture from cheap to expensive areas of the country or abroad. The fact that only a small number of families, predominantly Irish, have entered the market suggests that the need for long-distance travelling and the required capital outlay, plus competition from foreign (particularly Dutch) and domestic *gauje* dealers, restrict opportunities in the antique business. Carrying out tarmac surfacing of drives and paths is similar to antique dealing in that it requires long-distance migrations because the market in one city is rather limited, although this work is done occasionally by local families.

At this point, two features of the gypsy economy that have a bearing on official policy should be noted. The first is the obvious one, that all the activities discussed so far are market-oriented, making travellers economically dependent on cities. Yet, changes in the way the city is structured, politically and economically, make life more difficult for travellers in urban areas, and problems that arise from changes such as those occurring in the housing market are exacerbated by a particular prejudice against urban gypsies. Travellers in cities do not conform to the romantic, rural, stereotype, and they are often described in pejorative terms as 'tinkers', 'itinerants' or 'dropouts', ascriptions that are designed to dissociate them from 'real' gypsies. This prejudice contributes to an anti-urban bias in policy, discussed in chapter 9.

The second characteristic of the economy that affects policy is the distinction between occupations that require extensive travelling and those that can be carried on by sedentary or semi-nomadic gypsies. This results in the identification of nomadic travellers as a distinctive group, who tend to be more affluent than the others and who are not easily accommodated in a policy that emphasizes settlement. One practical problem is that they may not be included in local authority census estimates because of their migratory behaviour, so the need for sites will not reflect their occasional stays in an area — transit sites are rarely provided. More fundamentally, there is a mythology associated with them that is fostered by local travellers, among others, with whom they are competing for public funds. A prejudice against nomads is compounded by an ethnic prejudice, since most of the long-distance travellers are Irish. As Worrall (1979) notes, in discussing conflict in Swansea, 'invasions of Irish tinkers' are an important ingredient in the popular mythology. Not all Irish families in England and Wales travel long distances, however, nor are they all affluent; but the association is commonly made by groups who are hostile towards them. Apart from the ethnic association, this long-distance — local distinction creates a serious problem for central government, which is trying to gain acceptance at the local level for 'liberal' policies. Local administrations are more concerned with a 'solution' to a 'problem', that is, with the settlement of travellers and the control of inter-authority migrations — the practices of local authorities do not suggest acceptance of nomadism as a way of life.[5]

Agricultural work. Farm work is an exceptional activity for travellers in the sense that it is wage labour, which is generally avoided because it does not allow the gypsy to assume a dominant economic role. It has probably never been of more than seasonal importance for British gypsies, and opportunities diminish as more harvesting operations are mechanized. The principal sources of work have been the soft fruit crops in the Fens of eastern England, the West Midlands, Perthshire and Angus in Scotland, and the potato harvest. Travellers generally work on a casual basis in family groups and, while rates of pay are low, they can get a satisfactory return for a few weeks' work if most of the family is involved. Commonly, girls of 11 or 12 years of age or old people will look after the young children, freeing the rest of the family for work. The farmer also benefits from this system by avoiding payment of national insurance contributions.

While long-distance migrations to the biggest growing areas still occur, there has probably been a decline in agricultural migration during the last decade, not solely because of a contraction in demand. In east Yorkshire, for example, long-established seasonal movements to the potato and strawberry growing areas have largely been replaced by daily commuting of up to a range of 50 miles, while, since 1971, there has been a slight decline in the number of families undertaking farmwork. The harvest is no longer a fixed point in the annual work pattern, involving the whole community. Partly, this is due to agricultural work becoming economically marginal compared with work opportunities in the city, while the general reluctance to accept wage labour, which conflicts with the principle of economic autonomy, is greater when the returns are small. As one traveller commented to me

5 As an illustration of this point, the Gypsy Liaison Officer for Humberside attempted to prevent a group of long-distance travellers from entering the county on the grounds that they were not part of the county's population. His action was condemned as 'interference' by the National Gypsy Council.

when a farmer called at a site to hire workers, 'You only get the shit end of the stick.' A further change that is discouraging seasonal migrations is the increase in full-time education for traveller children. Some parents are unwilling to interrupt their children's education because of the value they attach to literacy training. At the same time, attendance at school reduces the number of workers in the family and so the economic gain from any sort of agricultural work is diminished.

The contraction of migrations for farm work has been misinterpreted. Cripps, for example, maintains that 'many gypsies are moving towards the towns as the opportunities for earning a livelihood in the countryside diminish' (Department of the Environment, 1976). This is a common misconception. Rather, what has happened is that seasonal migrations *away* from the towns have decreased both in distance and duration. Cripps's suggestion that British travellers are currently becoming urbanized is not just a factual error, however, but has ideological significance. I will enlarge on this issue in the next chapter.

The wealth-earning activities of British travellers described above do not constitute an exhaustive list; and, since they represent responses to the economy of the dominant society, they are likely to change as the structure of the British economy alters. These occupations are probably the most important ones in terms of the number of travellers involved, however, and currently they comprise most of the profitable ways of exploiting the dominant economic system. The essential feature of the traveller economy is not the specific occupations followed but the nature of the relationship with the larger society. Dominance, autonomy and flexibility are the salient characteristics.

Consumption

When compared with the standards of material comfort to which the dominant class in mainstream society aspires, the domestic economy of most British travellers is often taken as indicative of need. As I suggested in chapter 3, there is a tendency in official reports to make ethnocentric judgements about the material standards of travellers. I would argue that it is inappropriate to use conventional social indicators to measure need among travellers since they value different forms of material wealth to those considered desirable by house-dwellers.[6] In defining wealth or levels of well-being for the traveller community, it is essential to bear in mind the requirements of a life on the road, even for families that are no longer nomadic but continue the traditions of a nomadic life. More fundamental is the objective of minimizing contact with the dominant system where possible in order to maintain the boundary between gypsy society and the polluting *gaujes* − goods and services that can be supplied only by *gaujes* are avoided, beyond necessary transactions such as the purchase of food. The retention of autonomy can be recognized as an underlying objective even where it is difficult to achieve in practice.

An analysis of the consumption patterns of travellers is of particular relevance in an assessment of the impact of government policy. The kinds of provision made on official sites, for example, reflect mainstream standards and could be interpreted as an attempt to lessen perceived deprivation, but the application of inflexible standards is also designed to make sites more acceptable to the settled community − if travellers do not consume as much as house-dwellers and tend to improvise, they are judged to be deviant. Thus, the lessening of deprivation and the correction of deviance are confounded. The fact that gypsies do not necessarily conform when public funds are allocated to them in the form of well-equipped sites can be a source of disappointment to councillors and local authority officers, who believe their clients to be deprived and feel that the conception of gypsies as a social problem stems from this deprivation. This failure to conform then reinforces the view that they are deviant. Misconceptions such as this are based on an ethnocentric view of social well-being.

---

6 The problematic nature of social indicators has been recognized elsewhere; see, for example, Knox and Maclaren (1978), pp. 197−248.

Shelter and living space. Variation in the wealth of travelling people is expressed most clearly by the trailer. Most travellers in Britain now live in trailers rather than in wagons or bender tents,[7] and basic accommodation can be acquired very cheaply. In 1978, a poor family could buy a trailer for £100 or less. Trailers of this type usually originate on holiday caravan sites or are bought from *gauje* dealers, but are then traded several times within a gypsy community before being finally broken up for scrap and firewood. Families will exchange trailers every few years, usually buying a slightly more expensive model. The ease with which this cheap accommodation can be acquired is important for young couples who are starting families and it facilitates a high rate of family formation. As a result, the number of trailers accommodating the nuclear families constituting an extended family network can increase quite rapidly. In a typical family with ten children, of whom half are teenagers,[8] four or five new nuclear families might be formed within as many years, and this can cause considerable accommodation problems on official sites which are not designed to cater for expanding family networks. The availability of cheap trailers is also important in that low-income families in general can afford sound shelter that is cheap to heat and needs no maintenance. In the past, wagons were also traded among travellers at low prices, but the high prices offered for antique wagons encourages them to sell to *gauje* dealers and to buy a trailer with the proceeds. In any case, very few travellers in England and Wales now have wagons.

Affluence in the traveller community is generally indicated by an expensive, customized trailer. Standard traveller's trailers, built by a small number of firms in England, have distinctive chrome steel trimming on the exterior and can be embellished according to the customer's requirements. A typical model built by the Aaro Company of Hull sold for £6,568 in 1978 and, when customized, cost up to £8,000. A similar trailer built by Avalon Caravans of

---

7 Tents with frames made from branches and covered in rags. This was a common mode of shelter in the nineteenth century.

8 These figures are suggested by my own experience and may not apply elsewhere.

Hull varied in price from £7,000 to £12,000. A customized Astral, the most popular model in this price range for British travellers and of simple design, is now preferred to the more lavish, Baroque trailers that were produced in the 1960s and carried on the ornamental tradition of the wagon. It is worth noting that the price of the best trailers compares with that of a small terrace house outside a clearance area in a city like Leeds or Hull, although trailers, unlike houses, depreciate in value. It is certainly arguable that a travelling family has as high a standard of accommodation in an £8,000 trailer as they could obtain for the same price in the private housing market, while maintenance and heating costs are much lower.

With official sites becoming more numerous in England and Wales, however, we have to set against the low cost of shelter the rent charged for a pitch and services. In 1977 the model rent on permanent official sites was from £4 to £5 per week, ranging from £1.50 to £6 for a single pitch (Department of the Environment, 1977). A high proportion of gypsy families are large and require pitches for two trailers. Most authorities that have provided sites charge less than twice the single-pitch rent for a double pitch; where they do not, however, the rent is high, that is, comparable to rents charged for a council house, notwithstanding the fact that travellers provide their own shelter. For example, rents for double pitches were £12 in Liverpool and £10 in several London boroughs in 1977. By contrast, temporary sites, usually with minimal facilities such as a water tap and rubbish skip, were cheap, with rents ranging from nothing to £2.50. Thus, the economic benefits of travelling could be affected considerably by the availability and cost of sites, and we might question whether site provision represents a real increase in living standards as distinct from a politically expedient form of containment.

Transport. Motor vehicles are an essential part of the traveller economy and, like trailers, they are of importance as indicators of wealth and status. Among poor English gypsies, fairly old, small vans, Ford Transits and pick-up trucks predominate — they are adequate for transporting small quantities of scrap or for taking workers to seasonal harvesting jobs. In the Hull area, travellers appear to do all their own maintenance, with men often pooling their skills on a repair job, but if a vehicle is seriously defective, they break it up for scrap or spare parts. Dispensing with garages and *gauje* mechanics is consistent with the objective of minimizing dependence on mainstream society; it is also economically sensible, since families on low and irregular incomes could not afford garage charges, and it is possible because travellers have plenty of time to work on their vehicles. More affluent gypsies, who may be more specialized economically and may travel on inter-urban networks, have predictably larger and newer lorries than poor families, and may run a car in addition, with a Rolls Royce, Mercedes or Range Rover being characteristic status symbols for the richest families. Variations in the quality of vehicles and trailers together demonstrate conspicuous differences in affluence. However, it is generally true of English gypsy communities that vehicles are an important element of traveller culture, deriving from the economic need for mobility and the interest in vehicles as a source of scrap metal.

I do not have enough evidence to generalize about variations in mobility among British travellers, but among local travellers in the Hull area there are differences in mobility that relate to age, sex and income. Thus, there are a few families that are relatively immobile because no one in the family can drive — these are families that were living in horse-drawn wagons until a few years ago. This restricts work opportunities but not seriously, since other travellers provide transport to harvest areas or refuse tips, for example, and most young men will probably learn to drive. Very few women drive and several do not have access to a vehicle, so for hawking or shopping they use the bus or walk. This gives an advantage to the few women whose husbands drive them to towns away from the heavily worked areas for calling, and the removal of 25 families to a remote site outside the city has made shopping trips difficult for women without private transport. In other parts of England and Wales, variations in mobility may not be so marked. Around Sheffield, for example, women drive lorries on short trips for scrap collection (Gerald Capper, personal communication) and women drivers were conspicuous among affluent families fruit-picking in the Fens of eastern England in 1971. Immobility may be a problem for poor travellers, however, and the economic disadvantages resulting from immobility will be exacerbated by site development in areas remote from urban centres or public transport.

Other elements of domestic consumption. Without an understanding of the value system of travellers, it is difficult to distinguish those features of material culture that are symptoms of poverty and those that are culturally specific and reflect preferences rather than need. To illustrate the point, it will be useful to consider some details of the domestic economy. The use of cooking utensils, for example, demonstrates the need to define the cultural context if we are to decide whether or not provision is adequate. For many families, a frying pan, a large stew pot, a kettle and a teapot are the only items used regularly. Most food, if it needs preparation, is fried, and a stew, with pork or bacon, potatoes and cabbage, for example, provides a typical Sunday dinner. Children are given nearly all their food on a slice of bread, dispensing with the need for plates and cutlery. Keeping the equipment for food preparation and eating to a minimum is primarily an adjustment to travelling, a means of coping without the facilities enjoyed by most house-dwellers. If water has to be begged, it is essential to conserve it and to use as little as possible for washing up, while it is sensible in the restricted space of a trailer to manage without a lot of domestic equipment. These practical responses to travelling, combined with the more fundamental reluctance to become dependent on the larger society, account for many improvizations in domestic life. For example, I have seen a table knife used for chopping firewood and opening a tin of baked beans, in addition to its more usual functions. If the functional requirements of nomadism and the role of material objects in gypsy society are not recognized, however, such aspects of material culture might be taken as indicators of deprivation.

By contrast, there are items of domestic equipment that are highly valued by travellers that would be indicative of prosperity

in mainstream society but do not have the same economic significance in the gypsy community because the demands on income in
other respects, particularly for shelter, are much less. Thus, colour
television is now quite common, although it is also necessary to
have a portable generator to run it unless the family is on a permanent site where mains electricity is available. The combined cost
of colour television and generator would be beyond the means of
the poorest families, who would make do with a black-and-white
set run from car batteries. A colour television, however, is the kind
of non-essential good that occasional extra income gained on the
potato harvest or a scrap contract would be spent on, while a few
sedentary travellers can now obtain credit. A sophisticated music
centre or hi-fi system has similar priority to a colour television,
reflecting the importance of country and western music in traveller culture, and, again, the fairly recent adoption of the portable
generator makes it worthwhile to buy expensive equipment.
Another characteristic expression of wealth is Crown Derby china,
or a cheaper substitute in less affluent households.

These goods do not in themselves distinguish wealthy travellers
from the rest — cars, lorries and trailers are more important in this
respect. However, their absence in the trailers of the poorest families is notable. Cheap china, a radio and the portable black-and-
white television are characteristic possessions of low-income
families. The presence or absence of non-essential goods is of
limited significance in assessing wealth in the traveller community,
but material possessions do contribute to the formation of stereotypes. In particular, because gypsies do not appear to work for a
living or, at best, because their work is stigmatized as parasitic,
expressions of affluence support the view of the traveller as a
scrounger or someone whose sources of income are of doubtful
legality. The observation that travellers on illegal stopping places
do not pay rates is occasionally connected with the observation
that they watch colour television; the avoidance of house-dwellers'
obligation is considered unjust but the injustice is compounded if
travellers do well out of it. This attitude clearly conflicts with the
perception of travellers as a deprived community, and this accounts
for an ambivalence in popular and official reactions to them.

Production and consumption: a summary

This account of the occupations of British travellers and their domestic economy suggests the importance of the peripheral situation of gypsies in relation to both production and consumption. Work is peripheral in the sense that it is concerned either with resources that are classified as waste or residual by the dominant society or with gaps in supply. These two features of the economy are linked in the temporal pattern of work which reflects the irregular occurrence of opportunities created by the dominant system and the financial needs of travellers, which do not necessarily require regular inputs of labour and a regular income. It is interesting in this regard that British travellers are increasingly categorized as unemployed and thus eligible for social security benefits. This is indicative not of the decline of their own economy, but of the imposition of a classification on a culture in which to be employed or unemployed is a meaningless distinction. Unemployment benefit as an alternative to traditional forms of income, however, is compatible with a view of the larger society as exploitable. 'Signing on' cannot be interpreted as growing dependency, because the essential relationship between the gypsy community and the dominant system is not compromised.

Consumption patterns also reflect peripheral status in that there is a general tendency to minimize dependence on the goods and, particularly, the services of mainstream society. Beyond this, I would emphasize the flexibility in consumption patterns which make it possible for poor travellers to spend very little on some requirements, such as shelter and clothing, so that they have enough money for food (or a television), while at the same time affluent families may maximize expenditure on shelter and other goods. In regard to shelter, the insider—outsider comparison may be made in terms of the constraints on the family budget. Owing to the rigid structuring of the housing market in Britain, it is difficult to match shelter requirements and income. Within the limits imposed by trailer design, travellers can make closer adjustments to income than can members of the settled society.

These characteristics of the economy have important policy

implications. There is an opposition between the gypsy economy and the dominant economy from the mainsteam perspective, which centres on attitudes to resources and to the organization of work. The existence of this economy on the periphery of the larger society constitutes a threat — 'danger lies in marginal states' — because it challenges the categories that provide the secure base of the capitalist system. This threat has then to be countered by attempts to incorporate travellers into, or to exclude them from, mainstream modes of work and settlement.

MIGRATION

Migration is essentially a facet of economic organization — families do not usually move unless there is some apparent economic advantage to be gained from moving. Occasionally, however, there are other reasons for migration. Action by local authorities can be important, including harrassment and eviction, which is not necessarily malevolent (as, for example, when land is needed for redevelopment). Also, conflict within a traveller community may be resolved through one party leaving. Rather than thinking of these as alternative causes of migration, however, it is often the case that their effects combine. Harrassment by a local authority, for example, may combine with economic factors to encourage migration beyond the boundaries of the local authority; or, alternatively, harassment may foster local, tactical, moves if travellers, for social and economic reasons, have strong ties with an area. Short-distance moves, beyond the area designated in an order for the possession of land, can frustrate a council's eviction attempt. My experience suggests that there are specific economic, social or political reasons for virtually all moves, and Okely's suggestion (Adams *et al.*, 1975) that there is a migratory instinct or an ideology of travelling appears to me to obscure the rational basis of migration and, if anything, to contribute to the romantic myth and the image of deviance.

In Britain, it is possible to identify three spatial scales of migration: national (or international), regional and intra-urban. These migration fields can be associated with two types of traveller —

local and long-distance — with the former restricting their movements to a city region and the latter travelling primarily on an
inter-urban network. This dichotomy is suggested by my field
experience, but it is possible that it does not accommodate some
of the variants of travelling patterns. I cannot, however, reconcile
my information with Okely's threefold classification — sedentary,
travelled locally and travelled widely — because there is no apparent distinction in terms of economy and social networks
between sedentary families and local travelling families; stopping
for long periods in one location and undertaking short-distance
moves do not appear to be exclusive alternatives. While these
categories merge, there does appear to be a clear distinction
between those families moving or not moving within a city region
and long-distance travellers. As I suggested above, this distinction
has an economic basis, and it has considerable political significance.

Of particular interest in an assessment of the constraining effect
of the dominant system on gypsy culture are the changes that have
occurred in travelling patterns. The changes that are assumed to
have occurred in the last decade have a bearing on policy; for, if
change is interpreted as a transition from a rural to an urban
economy, it also suggests (for some) integration into the urban
system as an inevitable outcome. The problem of interpretation
can be illustrated with reference to a group of travellers in east
Yorkshire, where a marked contraction of the migration field has
occurred in the last two decades. About 20 years ago, travellers
based in Hull had a maximum range of travel of about 100 miles.
Destinations referred to include Mansfield, Retford, and Nottingham in the east Midlands; Wakefield and Harrogate in West Yorkshire; and Teesside to the north. By 1972, movement was confined
to a circuit that linked areas where seasonal farmwork was available, taking families up to 40 miles from Hull, with an additional
element of inter-urban moves, particularly to York and Gainsborough, Lincolnshire, where members of the same kin group had
permanent stopping places. By 1975, migrations to agricultural
areas in the west had ceased, leaving only movements between
Hull and York and within Hull; migrations for agricultural work
had been replaced by daily commuting.

Since most families now spend most of the year in the city it might be suggested that they have become urbanized, but the material basis of life has changed little during this period. Scrap metal dealing and farmwork have been important sources of income during the decade, and, while emphases have changed, the constant nature of the relationship between travellers and the dominant society is evident; there is no suggestion that contraction of the migration field has signified incorporation in the dominant system.

Two sets of factors have encouraged prolonged stays in the city. First, there are urban attractions, such as access to education and welfare services, which have discouraged extensive migration. While it would be premature to judge the impact of formal education, which has been available to the community only since 1972, it is notable that very few travellers who have acquired basic literacy have obtained a job in the mainstream economy, and then only for short periods. While this could be due to lack of appropriate skills, discrimination by employers or a slack labour market, there is clearly a lack of interest in permanent wage labour among teenagers, so education does not appear to be leading to incorporation in this sense. Parents have a strong interest in education for their children, although this is expressed exclusively in terms of the value of literacy, which is seen as useful in economic transactions with the dominant society and in dealing with the bureaucracy. Comments such as 'They can back you up' — that is, children can read the forms for you — and 'You don't have to let other people know your business' indicate the importance attached to literacy. Contradictory views are also expressed, however. One fairly affluent traveller told me that 'you don't have to be able to read or write to earn a penny or two', a sentiment that is consistent with Okely's finding that the most affluent travellers in her sample were the least literate (Adams *et al.*, 1975). It is possible that the wide acceptance of at least primary education, even when its utility is questioned, reflects a wish to deflect the social control agencies by seeming to conform. It is certainly evident that, while the availability of education has encouraged a sedentary life, it has not altered the terms of the gypsy–*gauje* relationship.

   The other factors that have contributed to the contraction of
the migration field and a more permanent association with the city
are primarily physical constraints and attractions that have
changed economic opportunities. These include the closure of
some traditional stopping places in rural areas and the simul-
taneous appearance of stopping places in Hull which could be
occupied on a long-term basis whether they were officially sanctioned or not. The relative security of illegal stopping places in the
city resulted partly from central government advice to local
authorities in the mid-1970s that they should not harrass gypsies if
permanent sites had not yet been provided. Thus, travellers were
brought closer to their principal sources of income while access to
rural areas for those wishing to continue seasonal agricultural work
was maintained by substituting commuting for migration.

   From this example, it is apparent that economic and institutional factors have combined to bring travellers into the city on a
more permanent basis without altering the essential elements of
their world-structure. They have not, therefore, become urbanized
in the conventional sense. In order to make this point with greater
conviction, however, it will be helpful to examine the urban
experience of travellers on an historical and cross-cultural basis.

CHAPTER 8

The urban association

Consider, first, the following observations about travellers in urban areas.

At the end of World War II, there were fewer than fifteen travelling families in the Dublin area. By 1961 there were forty-six and today there are eight times that number. [Gmelch, 1975]

The remorseless and often fast-moving tide of urban development has overtaken many traditional stopping places close to industrial areas. The consequences are the more devastating because so many gypsies are moving towards the towns as the opportunities of earning a livelihood in the countryside diminish. [Department of the Environment, 1976]

Cultural change seems irreversible; it is probable that this will be the last Itinerant generation to possess a distinctive subculture. [Kearns, 1977]

As economic and social marginals, travellers simply lack the resources and opportunity structure necessary to develop more innovative and, in the long run, more satisfactory responses to their environment. Employment is a case in point. If travellers were able to obtain and keep conventional jobs in the settled community, many of the problems which currently confront them would be eradicated or minimized, including the low self-esteem men experience as a result of their economic dependence on the settled society. . . . [Gmelch, 1977b]

We might conclude from these statements that the move to the city is a recent transition; that this move has disrupted a traditional, rural economy; and that this in turn has led to dependence on the dominant society. The solution to the problem, then, is to give travellers proper jobs.

Collectively, these quotations are consistent with the modernization model that pervades the literature on ethnic minorities in
capitalist societies. Such interpretations of the problems affecting
British and Irish travellers are very similar to comments on native
Americans in urban situations, by writers such as Graves (1970),
and Levy and Kunitz (1971). As Tipps (1973) has argued, those
who suggest that the embrace of urban society has devastating
consequences for indigenous minorities carry with them a cognitive map constructed from the familiar categories of urban,
industrial society, and this map is used inappropriately to chart
the course of minorities through the dominant system. As I
suggested in chapter 2, with reference to Giddens and Berger, the
argument hinges on the nature of social change and its significance
for groups that are outside the dominant mode of production. One
way by which the inadequacy of the modernization model can be
demonstrated with respect to travelling people is to examine the
historical association with cities. If it can be shown that residence
in the city is a long-established characteristic of the gypsy community, it will then be difficult to maintain that the move to the
city has been recent and traumatic. There is, in fact, considerable
evidence from Britain and, to a lesser extent, North America that
throws doubt on the modernization thesis.

It is plausible that travellers have become urbanized at the same
rate as the rest of the population because their economic adaptations require close proximity to markets and access to resources
generated by urban populations. Accordingly, we might expect to
find gypsy communities that have lived permanently in or near to
cities in Western Europe and North America at least since the
middle of the nineteenth-century, when the major industrial
societies became predominantly urban. It is difficult to establish
that this was generally the case because records of nineteenth-
century gypsy communities are sparse. The presence of gypsies in
cities that were growing rapidly in population, with foreign
migrants making a large contribution, as in North America, may
have been considered unremarkable by contemporary observers of
the urban scene. Also, if there was a popular association between
gypsies and rural areas, the ethnic identity of travellers in cities,

living as it were out of context, might not have been recognized. Notwithstanding their somewhat cryptic presence in the nineteenth-century city, however, there are some well documented instances of urban communities.

The clearest accounts of urban gypsies in Britain relate to London. Samuel (1973), discussing migratory workers in the nineteenth-century city, makes a number of references to travellers in the metropolis, mostly between 1870 and 1900, which together suggest that gypsies were resident in London both permanently and on a seasonal basis; that they lived in wagons, tents or houses; and that they occupied land and houses both on the urban periphery and near the centre of the city.

Inner-city stopping places included Battersea and Wandsworth. In 1900, the Battersea gypsies were camped on land near the Southwestern Railway viaduct and they stayed for about six months every year, 'from October to the flat racing season', while some families always occupied the site during the summer. There is a photograph of a family living in a Reading wagon[1] in a yard in Battersea in the 1870s, and continuity of this occupation is confirmed by Acton (1974), who refers to house-dwelling gypsies in the area in the 1960s who had been resident for two generations. In the adjacent borough of Wandsworth, there is a similar record of occupation since the nineteenth-century. Thus, Booth (1902), writing in 1900, noted that 'The gypsy poor, as a floating population, have long been here. They come to church to be married and on a recent Whit Sunday, the church was crowded for a gipsy wedding.' It is apparent from Booth's account that they formed a permanent, partly house-dwelling community:

He [a missionary] had in this district two colonies of gipsies, costers, flower sellers and the like. In Summer, the gipsies go to the fairs, and before the start for Epsom in the Derby week the place is pandemonium. The houses are many of them owned by the richer members of the clan; and room is found for vans, with wheels and without, in which the poorer members crowd. The gipsies regard their quarters as their castle. [Booth, 1902]

---

1 A type of wagon, or *vardo*, originally built by Dunton of Reading with a high arched roof and ribbed walls. Those built for more affluent families were richly carved and gilded. See Ward-Jackson and Harvey (1972).

Here, as elsewhere in London, Booth associated gypsies with the poorest residential areas — 'the lowest class' and 'very poor' in his classification of status. Thus, in connection with travellers in Wandsworth, he writes:

Wardley Street and Lydden Grove are perhaps the worst of these low streets, and our own notes concerning the former read: Houses two storeyed, most of them flush with the pavement, a low common lodging house on one side and a yard full of wheelless gipsy vans on the other, each inhabited by a family. [Booth, 1902]

A number of other inner-city locations are referred to in contemporary reports, although the references are sometimes to people 'like gypsies', so that we cannot be certain that they were travelling people. These possible inner-city areas include Owen's Yard, Lambeth (1861), under the arches of London Bridge (1869), and Lisson Grove, in the Maida Vale area of northwest London (the latter reference in Booth, 1902).

Samuel also lists a number of stopping places on the urban fringe, namely Charlton, Plumstead, West Kensington, Hackney Wick, and Finsbury Park, and refers to house-dwelling gypsies in Canning Town and Deptford, which were close to the Essex and Kent countryside, respectively. 'Gypsies ended their autumn journeys on the outer peripheries of town . . . but, as the weather grew more severe, some of them moved further in, and went to live in rooms.'

The best documented stopping place on the edge of the city was Notting Dale, a part of the Borough of Kensington near the West London Junction Railway and the farms and brickfields of Wormwood Scrubs. As Booth described it,

The Potteries, which occupied part of the ground known as Notting Dale, seemed to have been built on an isolated estate only accessible along a narrow muddy lane . . . the district has for long been the resting place for tramps entering London from the North and West, and gipsy blood is very evident amongst the children in the schools and noticeable even in the streets. [Booth, 1902]

According to Samuel, this area was settled initially by refugee pig-keepers from Marble Arch and occupied subsequently by travelling people — primarily one kin group, the Hearnes. There is a print, dating from the late nineteenth-century, showing their wagons by the roadside. Booth confirms that the district was populated by inward movement from the provinces and outward movement that resulted from the clearance and improvement of inner-city areas, creating 'perhaps an unexampled concourse of the disreputable classes', with a social mix possibly similar to that of the *bidonvilles* of Paris, where there are also established gypsy communities. In 1898 the death rate in this area was 45.5 per thousand and the infant mortality rate 419 per thousand, and Booth coloured five streets in Notting Dale black on his social status map, indicating 'the lowest class'.

An interesting facet of London's social geography in the nineteenth-century which made the city suitable for settlement by travellers was the existence of a number of enclaves and exclaves like Notting Dale, which were, according to Booth, effectively outside the control of the authorities. He refers, for example, to 'a curious patch beside the Great Eastern Railway to the north of Hackney Downs', which was an isolated area of poverty, accessible only from one side, and, similarly, a district surrounded by a meander of the River Lea, called Orchard House: 'The place has been a sort of Alsatia for dock thieves; the people are said to be by nature piratical and predatory. It is so remote that a policeman is seldom seen in it, and 25 minutes would be needed to fetch one from Poplar.[2]

Chesney (1970) makes specific reference to Irish travellers in London, which suggests that their acquaintance with cities may not be so recent as writers on travellers in Ireland have maintained. With reference to an unnamed contemporary source, he says that:

In Victorian times, these people of Irish origin formed at least the hard core of the vagrant tinkers. For some years after the mid-century, Shelta is said to have been so common that it was virtually impossible to take a walk through a London slum without hearing it spoken. [Chesney, 1970]

---

2 Was the Victorian city closer to the anarchist ideal of Bookchin, Sennett, or Colin Ward than the modern British city?

Similarly, D. Smith (1975) mentions accounts of Irish travellers in Bath and Liverpool in the late nineteenth-century.

Reports of settlement in other British cities confirm the pattern. In Liverpool, for example, waste ground on the edge of the built-up area in Everton was used as a camp in 1879 and was still in existence in 1886, despite summonses for contravening a public health act (Samuel, 1973). Conversations with travellers in Hull indicate that their use of the city at the beginning of the century was similar to that suggested by Booth's surveys of London. They rented small houses in the inner city, mostly in streets that are now part of the central area and have been redeveloped for commercial uses. They rented accommodation during the winter months, keeping their wagons in yards, and returned to the road in the spring. Some families, however, would stay for several years in a house. Alternatively, they spent the winter on the edge of the city, on farms or on roadside verges. It is evident that contact with the city has been uninterrupted at least since 1900. Similarly, Worrall (1979) refers to a family in Swansea that has been resident in the city for 155 years.

In North America, a similar long association with cities is probable, although the evidence is rather more limited than for Britain and most of it refers to the more recent past. One report suggesting an established presence appeared in the *New York Herald* in 1895:

Prince Williams, leader of the Connecticut gypsies, died in East Hartford, owning an hotel and real estate there, and other property worth more than $100,000, acquired by horse dealing. He was 62 years old, came from Devonshire 40 years ago and was 20 years in East Hartford. He systematically travelled in the summer and the fall in handsome, well-equipped wagons. [Crofton, 1908]

Harney and Troper (1975), in an account of migrations to Canadian cities between 1890 and 1930, note that, while some gypsies travelled in rural areas around Toronto, others moved straight to the city and were permanently resident, renting dilapidated store fronts close to the city centre for fortune-telling and dealing in cut-price goods. By the 1920s, gypsies were living with other ethnic minorities on Maxwell and Halstead Streets in Chicago (Brown, 1924), while Oujevolk (1935), in an anecdotal paper in the *Journal of the Gypsy Lore Society*, describes a group of Kalderas gypsies (Russian coppersmiths) 'living on a dirty little street called Hudson Avenue, in the main business section of Brooklyn' (in 1934). Oujevolk also referred to gypsy communities in Trenton and Jersey City, New Jersey. The dates of some of these references do not conflict with a suggestion by Gropper (1975) that there was a transition from rural to urban areas in the 1920s and 1930s, but she produces no firm evidence for this and her book fits into the mould of the modernization literature. It is likely that some gypsies settled initially in cities, as in Toronto, either permanently or on a seasonal basis, adapting to the dominant society in the same way as they had done in Europe. Others probably travelled in rural areas until it was seen that an urban location offered greater economic opportunities.

THE PROBLEM OF VISIBILITY

In suggesting that the recognition of a recent rural—urban transition is consistent with the modernization model, I have implied that the facts have been selected to fit the model. It is evident, however, that travellers have become a conspicuous minority in cities only in recent decades and so their presence is more likely to have been recorded. Statistical evidence, in other words, could be a product of changing social attitudes to the minority, and in Britain this recognition coincides with their emergence as a political problem requiring central government initiative. A comparison of the urban experience of gypsies in Britain and North America suggests that their recent arrival in British cities could be accounted for by changes in the housing market and by urban land use policies which have increased their visibility. The fact that North American gypsies are largely hidden from the view of the larger society and that the British and North American housing markets operate rather differently suggests that the urban environment is of crucial importance in accounting for the difference in status.

In Britain, changes in the housing market, in tenure categories and in the composition of the housing stock, coupled with a series of acts that have increased local authority control over the use of land, have effectively strengthened the boundary between travellers and the rest of society, making attributions of deviance more likely. In 1900 about 90 per cent of all households lived in private rented accommodation; by 1947 the proportion of households renting privately had fallen to 61 per cent, owner occupation had risen to 26 per cent, but the proportion in local authority housing was still quite small — 13 per cent. By 1972, however, owner occupation and local authority tenancy together dominated the market, with 47 and 33 per cent, respectively (Elliott, 1978). Baker and O'Brien (1979) describe an almost identical trend in Ireland. This decline in the private rented sector has contributed to the general problem of homelessness in British cities and has greatly restricted access to housing for gypsies because the eligibility rules of building societies and local authority housing managers effectively exclude most travellers. The flexibility of the housing system has been lost, and with it its adaptative potential for travellers. Other changes have exacerbated the problem. The redevelopment of nineteenth-century residential areas has taken away storage space for wagons and trailers; town planning legislation, with an emphasis on single-use zoning, has made the use of land by travellers more conspicuously non-conforming; and there are far fewer non-gypsy itinerants than there were in the nineteenth-century, so the travellers' life-style is more obviously deviant.[3] These changes suggest that the urban environment has become more strongly classified, in Bernstein's terms; and the stronger the classification, the less likely it is that mixing of categories will be tolerated. Thus, I would argue that travellers have emerged as a uniquely deviant urban minority because of structural changes in cities.

It is interesting in this regard that the Association of Metro-

---

3   Harney and Troper (1975) describe a large number of itinerant, non-gypsy traders in Toronto at the turn of the century. Flora Thompson, in *Lark Rise to Candleford*, makes a similar observation about rural England during this period.

politan Authorities (AMA), when it was considering site provision for travellers in 1974, had no conception of gypsies as an urban minority. It was suggested that the urban 'problem' was growing because people were moving from slum clearance areas 'into the caravan way of life and adopting the work habits of the itinerant community' (AMA, 1974). The problem is, rather, that most travellers who have not been provided with a permanent site have no option but to stop on vacant land in the city, whereas early in the century the urban environment could absorb them. Given that there are now considerable constraints on travellers living in urban areas, it is impossible to accept Acton's (1974) free-market argument. He maintains that 'To predict . . . the change in the relative costs of housedwelling and travelling is not too difficult. If we go on from there to assume that . . . the net effect of individual choices will be to equalize average marginal rewards in the two different modes of residence, then we need only make in addition some estimate of the demand for gypsies' services in order to be able to predict the gypsy population.' This is singularly unrealistic.

The problems affecting British gypsies can be put into perspective by comparing their status with that of gypsies in the United States. They are concentrated in the largest metropolitan areas, and, as in Europe, they occupy an economic niche that keeps them outside the wage labour system. The communities described by Sutherland (1975) in the San Francisco Bay area, and by Gropper (1975) in New York, are Kalderas gypsies, who, traditionally, were skilled at rivetless metalworking and had a monopoly of repair work on copper laundry vats and other copper utensils. When laundries installed stainless steel vats, the gypsies shifted to fender (bumper) repairs which required minimal equipment, namely a hammer, and to other work requiring little capital outlay, such as mending supermarket trolleys, drive surfacing, roof repairing and selling plastic flowers. The similarity with the British traveller economy in the sense that it creates minimal dependence on the larger society is apparent. Fortune-telling is the other principal occupation, which has resulted in some conflict with authority where it is illegal, in New York City and Chicago, for example. The market for all these services is very limited, and in order to secure a steady income extended families or coalitions of extended families form a *kumpania,* which Sutherland defines as a persistent unit of economic and social organization which attempts to maintain territorial monopoly in exploiting the *gaujes,* principally by controlling fortune-telling licences. This involves some bargaining with authority in order to secure the position of the *kumpania* and to deter any other families, who would be reported to the police for any illegal activity. A further important element in the gypsy economy is welfare, but, as Sutherland explains, this does not represent any erosion of gypsy autonomy. 'On the contrary, welfare is to them an incredible stroke of luck, yet further proof of the guillibility of the *gaje*' (Sutherland, 1975).

Although their economic relationship to mainstream society is essentially the same as that of British travellers, unlike the latter, American gypsies are an inconspicuous minority and not a particular target for the social control agencies. The main reason for this is that they live in rented houses, primarily in low-income areas, so that, outwardly, their culture does not appear different to that of other ethnic minorities living in the same areas. For this reason, they are not labelled as deviant. One gypsy community in the San Francisco Bay area, for example, lives in 'a depressed town of substandard housing, its most noticeable feature being the maze of railway tracks that form the natural boundaries for the various ethnic groups, Blacks, Mexican Americans, Indians, and poor Whites' (Sutherland, 1975). Most of the housing had been condemned under urban renewal projects and the gypsies were able to adapt the area to their social needs by occupying houses in close proximity to each other, retaining the essential extended family network, and, by removing interior walls, making a space similar to the interior of a trailer. The only conflict with authority connected with their way of life involved occasional violations of garbage regulations.

Sutherland's research demonstrates that American gypsies can adapt the city to their needs; and, while there is an ideological boundary between gypsies and the larger society, there are few, if any, physical boundaries to reinforce their ethnic identity. Cities in the United States are less structured than British cities in the sense that there are fewer institutional constraints on residence in a particular area, although there are considerable economic constraints. Thus, gypsies have a greater opportunity to adjust to the built form of the city; there is a closer similarity between the status of gypsies in the United States today and in the nineteenth-century city in Britain than there is between modern British gypsies and urban American communities. This is not to deny that institutions have a role in structuring residential space in the United States (see, for example, Harvey, 1974), but the constraints imposed by institutions do not have adverse affects on gypsies compared, say, with blacks. The obvious contrast with British cities is that a much higher proportion of residential accommodation is privately rented and an insignificant proportion of housing is provided by the public sector, so that eligibility rules that incorporate social criteria are not such an important factor in the allocation of residential space. Thus, the American housing system is more flexible, and this works to the advantage of gypsies.

In making this comparison between Britain and North America and between gypsy communities in the nineteenth-century British city and the modern city, it is evident that there is a consistent connection with low-income areas. This might prompt a question about the class position of gypsies, discussed in a general sense in chapter 2. The association with the poorest groups in American society led Kornblum and Lichter (1972) to conclude that gypsies were, in Oscar Lewis's terms, a part of 'the culture of poverty'. (Kornblum made the same connection in his study of Boyash gypsies in a *bidonville* in an industrial suburb of Paris[4].) They asserted that 'in the city, the gypsies are the princes of the Lumpenproletariat'. However, as Marx used the term 'lumpenproletariat', he was referring to that residual part of the working class that was only occasionally in employment and whose status resulted from the exploitation of labour by the capitalist class. For the gypsy community, however, residence in a poor area provides a

---

4 Boyash gypsies originated in the Balkans and speak a Romanian dialect. Traditionally, they are associated with animal training and the circus. The *usari*, or bear trainers, travelled widely in Europe early in the present century. For an account of the Boyash in Paris, see Kornblum (1975).

means of keeping outside the system and constitutes a source of cheap *gauje* labour — it does not signify a structurally determined dependency. Poor housing, for example, may be seen by travellers as adaptable space, and its occupation does not reflect status in mainstream terms. Marginal space, like Notting Dale, may be occupied by the residual labour force, but for the gypsies it provides a base for the exploitation of the dominant society. Terms like 'lumpenproletarian' and 'marginality' are applied to travellers because they appear to be a group that is exploited by the capitalist system, and this exploitation confers on them residual status. While travellers are exploited in some ways, their capacity to exploit is obscured by inclusion in the lumpenproletarian category, and it is this capacity that explains their adaptations to the urban environment.

CHAPTER 9

The official response

The true gypsy is a wonderful person.
Lord Brooke of Cumnor

Among Western industrialized societies, there are considerable variations in the governmental response to travelling people. This variation may be ascribed to the level of visibility of gypsies as a non-conforming minority, discussed in the last chapter, and to the combined effects of social attitudes to land use (specifically, socially acceptable levels of disorder in the built environment), and government policies in the fields of housing, land use planning, and the provision of social services. Clearly, the degree to which travellers are recognized as a conspicuously different minority is bound up with these political and social attributes of the larger society. Essentially, we would expect that in a highly regulated society gypsies would be conspicuous, they would be identified in political terms as a problem and would be a target for control policies; whereas in societies where the government has a looser grip on non-conformists, and generally exercises less control over the housing and land markets, gypsies would merge with the background to the extent that the majority of the population might be unaware of their existence. The comparison between Britain and the United States suggested that these were the two basic variants but this is probably an over-simplification. A few other examples suggest other forms of adaptation and response. Thus, in Sweden, where social policy is based on the assumption that there is consensus and an acceptance of conformity, gypsies are relatively inconspicuous because most of them live in apartments and have accepted a superficial conformity. There is little conflict with the rest of society. In Holland, by contrast, a pluralistic approach has been adopted by the government, with the provision of caravan sites under a 1968 act, and this has resulted in the strengthening of the boundaries between travellers and the rest of society. Some of the sites are virtually autonomous zones, being large and subject to little control (Connell, 1976), but illegal camping is a source of social conflict. France and Italy provide another variant in that the shantytowns, particularly in Paris and Rome, provide hospitable environments and the settlement of travellers is not generally a political issue. We could represent the problem diagramatically as follows:

INTEGRATION   MAXIMUM CONFLICT/   ADAPTATION
               MAXIMUM VISIBILITY

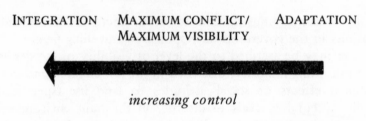

increasing control

DEPENDENCE   AUTONOMY

According to this conception of the political issue, conflict is greatest where the culture of the minority, by comparison with that of the larger society, makes it non-conforming but where integration, as a policy objective, has not been realized. Conflict is least where resources contributing to the economy and social welfare of the minority, such as housing, are least subject to central control and allocation. Visibility will be low where there is no alternative but to conform or where gypsies are not recognized as a minority requiring regulation. In the former case, it is difficult to know whether integration and dependence are appropriate terms to describe social and economic status, since gypsies may develop strategies to resist state control and conformity may be only superficial. The following account of the government's response to travelling people in England and Wales fits into the middle ground in this scheme. There is no discernible shift over time towards integration or autonomy, but it is evident that these conflicting objectives have contributed to the debate at central government level. I will concentrate here on the development of policies in Parliament and will explore the consequences of legislation at the local level in the next chapter.

CENTRAL GOVERNMENT POLICY

Debates on travelling people in the British Parliament have been concerned almost exclusively with the problem in England and Wales. There have been occasional questions in the House of Commons about Scottish travellers, but legislation drawn up in the Commons has not applied to Scotland because of differences in the legal system. I will comment briefly on references to gypsies during the 1940s and 1950s, when conflicts between travellers and the settled population first gave rise to official concern and a campaign for special provision for travellers was initiated by the Kent MP, Norman Dodds. With this background, we can examine in greater detail the passage through Parliament of the Caravan Sites Bill in 1968 and its consequences for travellers and local authorities.

There are several consistent features of parliamentary discussions on this issue, at least until 1968. First, arguments were based, inevitably, on very little information about gypsy culture, and there were a number of persistent myths that coloured the debate, notably the 'real gypsy' myth. Second, there was a presumption that travellers were concentrated in the South-East of England and that there was no problem for local authorities in the North. Third, there was a rural bias in discussions, which lent support to the real gypsy myth. As I suggested in chapter 2, gypsies have been associated with nature to the extent that they are seen as a part of nature. To give a bizarre example of this racialist conception, in 1952 an application was made to Kent County Council by Lady Hart Dyke of Lullingstone Castle to provide a site for thirty *Romany* families in the castle grounds. The families were to have been specially picked so that their wagons would add to the picturesqueness of the locality (Fraser, 1953). This view had serious consequences for travellers, since there was a presumption by members of Parliament that gypsies should be excluded from cities and that many of those who were in cities were not gypsies — a racial myth provided the rationale for an exclusionary policy.

THE EMERGENCE OF THE 'GYPSY PROBLEM' IN PARLIAMENT

In June 1947 the Minister of Health, Aneurin Bevan, was asked about the numbers of gypsies and 'vagrants' in the country and their inclusion in the National Health scheme. The minister conceded ignorance about numbers but said that every effort would be made to include them in the National Health scheme. Following this early concern for incorporation in the welfare state, no interest in travellers was evident until the debates initiated by Norman Dodds, who was concerned specifically with harrassment by local authorities and with site provision. It should be noted that Dodds, who gained a reputation as a champion of travelling people, subscribed to the real gypsy myth, and it was this undefinable group whose interests he was concerned with. The racial mythology may have been fostered in the post-1945 period by the existence of a large number of homeless families, some of whom, it was claimed, were living in gypsy camps — an unlikely association. Dodds also made it clear that he believed that a long-term solution to the problem lay in integration with the settled community. His concern, however, was genuine enough.

Initially, his questions were met with complacency and inaction. In April 1951, when he accused the local authorities and the police of persecuting travellers, the parliamentary secretary to the Minister of Local Government and Planning was clearly offended. He claimed there was no persecution and resented the inference that there was (House of Commons, 1951b). Earlier, the Minister for Planning, Hugh Dalton, had argued that local authorities' need to put land to its 'best and most effective use' took

priority over the needs of travellers, and if this policy led inciden-
tally to the harrassment of gypsies it was no concern of the central
government (House of Commons, 1951a). Similarly, when in 1952
Dodds raised the question of evictions by councils in the West
Midlands, which were causing considerable distress, the minister
(Harold Macmillan) replied, 'I should hardly have thought that a
borough (that is, an urban area) was the best place for gypsy
caravans' (House of Commons, 1952). Throughout the 1950s
and the early 1960s, evictions continued, but there was no initiative in Parliament to make special provision for travellers and so
legalize their status. In fact, several acts worsened their position,
particularly the Caravan Sites and Control of Development Act,
1960, which ensured that travellers would no longer be able to
buy land for private sites, and the 1959 Highways Act, which
specifically discriminated against gypsies who camped in the curti-
lage of a highway.

THE BACKGROUND TO THE 1968 ACT

The problem resurfaced in the 1960s. Attention was initially
focused on Kent, probably because members from London-
suburban and rural constituencies in this county were being pres-
sed by their constituents to 'do something' about travellers
camped on roadsides and in proximity to residential areas. In 1967
there was a debate on gypsies which was concerned almost exclusively with Kent, and all except one of the participants in the
debate represented the London suburbs, the exception representing Ashford, an expanded town. (For a discussion of this issue, see
Acton, 1974.) The government had asked local authorities for
information on travellers, and the returns suggested a regional
concentration in southern England and the West Midlands. In fact,
the Joint Parliamentary Secretary to the Minister of Housing and
Local Government averred that 'it would seem that the plurality
of counties have no problem at all'. Thus, it appeared reasonable
at the time to concentrate attention on Kent. The traveller population was believed to be largest here, and local MPs were conscious

of conflict with the settled population. The illusion that most travellers lived in the West Midlands and Kent led to a further illusion, namely, that Kent was acting as a magnet for travellers from much of southern England. The member for Ashford, William Deedes, made this assertion on the grounds that there was an apparent tripling of the county's population between 1962, when the county council conducted a census, and 1966, an increase that he attributed to the fact that Kent had made some progress with site provision and these sites were attracting large numbers of travellers from elsewhere. Deedes cited a Kent County Planning Committee report for 1966 which said that they had no wish to see Kent become a national reception centre for gypsies, and he accepted this as fair comment. Given the gross inaccuracy of the national survey conducted in 1965, however, it is probable that one or both of Kent's estimates was in error and that the increase in population was largely a product of bogus statistics. Also, the idea of movements of travellers *en masse* to official sites is unconvincing in the light of recent research, which indicates that the migration patterns of most English travellers are highly localized. The notion of gypsies being a rootless, migratory ethnic group is another myth that informs the official response. The important point about the official perception of the problem in Kent, however, is that this county appeared to be a special case where action was warranted, and this change from complacency to concern indicated a significant shift in attitude.

The outcome of the Kent debate was only that the government agreed that local authorities should co-operate in providing sites. While the ministry was concerned that an adequate number of sites should be provided, it was equally concerned to control the activities of travellers, for example, by using the Civic Amenities Act to prevent gypsies salvaging derelict cars — the malignant element of steel production. The debate was also instructive in that it revealed the basis of Eric Lubbock's concern for the problem; for it was Lubbock, the member for Orpington, who introduced the Caravan Sites Bill in the Commons in 1968, legislation that was initially considered to be liberal and pluralist. However, in the Kent debate, Lubbock claimed that 'we have far too many caravans in our borough'; people were writing to him all the time asking for action and several hundred people had demonstrated in favour of evictions by the London Borough of Bromley. In fact, Lubbock's comments could not be distinguished from other negative arguments, and it is evident that the hostility of the electorate towards travellers was the principal concern of all Kent MPs. Beyond this, William Deedes advocated housing and integration as a long-term policy, but, to his credit, he was the only speaker to question whether the disturbance caused by travellers in a tidy environment was a reflection on the larger society or on the travellers.

THE CARAVAN SITES BILL

The arguments over Part 2 of Eric Lubbock's Caravan Sites Bill, in particular at the second reading in March 1968 and in the committee stage, demonstrate a consistency of attitudes towards travellers. Not surprisingly, the 1967 report, *Gypsies and other Travellers*, had done little to correct prejudices. In general, members of Parliament were no more knowledgeable than they had been in the 1950s — legislation was enacted on the basis of established myths.

In introducing the bill at the second reading (House of Commons, 1968a), Lubbock reflected the prevalent view of travellers. Referring to his own constituency, he expressed concern about the visible products of the gypsy economy, claiming that travellers were creating the most appalling mess with their car-breaking. He saw permanent sites as a means of controlling this activity. In the long run, he argued, it may be that, as gypsies settle down on the new sites, they will turn to other work — 'Every encouragement should be given them by the local authorities to do so.' Meanwhile, he envisaged that sites would be able to contain 'the more offensive occupations' of travellers. This argument was consistent with Lubbock's assimilationist position. He suggested that the population would become static, again in the long run, but that the desire for mobility would remain 'until a new generation had been through schools and become assimilated with the general population *and* set up their own households in ordinary accommodation'. Elsewhere in the debate, Lubbock suggested that permanent sites would allow travellers to continue their traditional way of life, but the weight of his argument was clearly on the side of regulation and assimilation.

Among the more enlightened comments, we might note:

1. a criticism by John Wells (Maidstone) of the statistics contained in the government report 'which tend to be quoted as reliable for generations afterwards': he noted the seasonal shift in occupations, which rendered meaningless the 52 per cent of families giving scrap-dealing as their occupation. This scepticism may be compared with the confidence expressed by Arthur Skeffington (Joint Parliamentary Secretary) that the figures for gypsies *had been established* by the ministry's survey, and a similar expression of confidence by Lubbock. He suggested that the survey had shown that there were very few gypsies in county boroughs (larger urban areas, excluding London) so that they should be under no obligation to provide sites. Other speakers pointed out that some county boroughs did, in fact, have substantial populations;

2. a comment by James Davidson (Aberdeenshire West) that the denigration of Irish travellers by several speakers was racialist, an accusation made also by the member for Nottingham West, who objected to the use of the term 'gypsy' in the clause providing eviction powers were adequate sites had been provided.

Informed comment was clearly outweighed by ignorance and prejudice. The real gypsy myth was used repeatedly to justify attacks on travellers in general. Thus, Gwilym Roberts (South Bedfordshire) used the term 'mobile spivs' and expressed the hope that 'if we have controlled sites, they will be controlled in a real sense'. Similarly, James Allason (Hemel Hempstead) objected to scrap dealing — 'I would have thought that by the 1970s we should have ceased to break up cars in this disgusting way' — and he advocated the use of social workers to persuade travellers 'to accept the normal decencies of British life'. He also feared that site provision would lead to Irish travellers 'flooding into the country'

and that, 'if too many sites were provided, nomadism would continue to the detriment of children's education and civilizing influences'. One of the Bill's sponsors, A. H. Macdonald (Chislehurst)
commented in the same vein:

It is the way of life which may be criticised. It is wrong for people to travel
around like what one honourable member described as 'mobile spivs' without
paying rent, rates, or taxes. . . . We are not talking of specific acts, so much,
although these are offensive, but of a way of life which is incompatible with
that chosen by the rest of us. . . .

Thus, the Bill was launched in a climate of intolerance and this
view is confirmed by the discussion at the committee stage, where
more considered argument might have been expected (House of
Commons Standing Committees, 1967–8). The main point of
interest was the provision of workplaces on sites which concerned
several committee members. It is notable that the members for
South Bedfordshire and Hemel Hempstead, who had both made
intemperate speeches during the second reading, were concerned
about the conjunction of residence and workplace on sites – a
major point of conflict between mainstream society and travellers.
Thus, Gwilym Roberts argued: 'I am all for providing these people
with decent, health-controlled sites and also for providing them
with the means of carrying on their occupation, but it is essential
that these two things should be done separately.' Following a
ritual denunciation of travellers, the member for Hemel Hempstead expressed concern about children playing on sites where car-
breaking was carried on. 'It is', he said, 'highly undesirable that
they should have car-breaking as part of their daily curriculum.
. . . I am sure it is right that these two things should be entirely
divorced.' This led Eric Lubbock to remind the committee that
the legislation would not require local authorities to provide work
space, and he implied that they should not be encouraged to do
so, because that might deter travellers from taking up other
occupations and lead them to persist in their traditional way of
life. Further, he argued that, when provision was made for scrap-
breaking, the land so used should be located in an industrial area

allocated in the development plan. All three proponents of segregation illustrate nicely the association between a restricted code, with an abhorrence of the mixing of categories, and assimilationist thinking. The only dissent from this view was expressed by John Farr (Harborough), who appreciated the advantages of combining workplace and residence: 'They cannibalise cars or decimate them, or whatever they do, and pop inside the caravan for a cup of tea.' One positive outcome of the committee's deliberations was a recommendation that the requirement to provide sites should be extended to county boroughs who could, however, claim exemption if they had no record of gypsies stopping in their areas in the previous five years or no suitable land, a clause that led to an interesting pattern of official denial of a local gypsy population.

When the Bill went back to the Commons (House of Commons, 1968b), the view of the legislation as an instrument for controlling and incorporating the minority was reinforced by the proposed amendments. No one, in fact, suggested that the Act might impose undue constraints on travellers. The member for Harborough argued for larger sites than the 15-pitch limit laid down for London and the county boroughs because the necessary measure of supervision and control would be possible only on larger sites. This amendment was negatived but could have worked to the advantage of travellers because it is likely that supervision would be more difficult on a large site. More radically, Wells suggested exempting those councils that were making 'better steps' than providing sites, that is, putting travellers in houses. The member for Chislehurst objected to a further proposal by Wells to oblige local authorities to house gypsies, not because this was intrinsically wrong but because integration was a long-term process and ought not to be rushed into. It is evident from this, and from other arguments advanced in the Commons, that sites were widely construed as an intermediate step to housing.

In July 1968 the Caravan Sites Bill was debated in the House of Lords (House of Lords, 1968a, 1968b, 1969). The discussion in the upper house revealed other dimensions of the problem and was characterized by views that were perceptibly more liberal than those expressed in the Commons, possibly reflecting the detachment of their lordships from the electorate. In general, however, the draft of the Bill met with approval. Two aspects of policy of particular interest were the establishment of sites in cities and the effect of site development of nomadism.

On the question of provision in urban areas, Craigmyle objected that a statutory limit of 15 pitches in London and the county boroughs could be inconsistent with the requirement to provide 'adequate accommodation'. While not disagreeing with this view, Lord Kennet, who introduced the Bill in the house, argued that the 15-pitch limit was a compromise — the anti-urban bias of the Bill's sponsors accounted for the initial exemption of London and the county boroughs; the county authorities objected to this so the limited requirement for the cities was introduced. The county boroughs were still hostile to the Bill, however, and Lord Milverton, representing the views of the Association of Municipal Corporations, made the dubious point that scarcity of land in cities ruled out site provision. 'Towns', he said, 'are surely not appropriate places for these sites.'

Nomadism did not appear to present a problem. Lord Kennet, accepting the fiction that there were 15,000 gypsies in England and Wales, hoped that enough sites would be provided to allow travellers free movement between them, and he was against enforced assimilation: 'it should not be any object of our social policy to compel or press any gypsy who does not want to settle down to do so'. Exceptionally, Lord Craigmyle appreciated the stability of migration patterns and their seasonal nature and wondered how short-term stopping places would be interpreted under the terms of the Act, which required site provision for travellers 'resorting to' an area. Again, Kennet expressed the hope that sites would be so numerous that the question of interpretation would not arise. In fact, none of the contributors to the parliamentary debates anticipated the level of local hostility to gypsy sites, and the obstructive attitude of many local authorities, which led to a very slow rate of site provision in the decade after the Act came into force.

These contributions, while idealistic, were at least sympathetic to gypsy culture. The racial myth had an airing, however, in an

irrelevant speech by Lord Willis: 'I should find it extremely sad if
we could not do something to save that rare and rich culture, to
separate in some way the true Romany from all the hangers on.
. . .' Willis was, however, challenged by Lord Donaldson of Kings-
bridge, who maintained that persecution was wrong, 'even though
their pedigree may not be good enough for my noble friend'.

The debates on Part II of the Caravan Sites Bill provide little
support for the pluralist thesis. Despite the euphoria of gypsy
organizations when the Act came into effect in 1970 (according to
Acton, 1974), it is clear that the legislation was intended primarily
as a measure of control to satisfy the demands of the settled
population. The sponsoring MPs were strongly influenced in their
views to 'do something about the problem'. There is little evidence
that the Bill's supporters, including Eric Lubbock, believed that
the traveller economy and culture should be accommodated by
the larger society. Rather, sites were seen as a short-term expedient for resolving conflict, with integration into the dominant
system as the long-term objective.

IMPLEMENTATION OF THE ACT

Following the royal assent for the Caravan Sites Act, there was
two years of inaction. The government would not implement Part
II on the grounds of financial stringency; yet, as Eric Lubbock
pointed out in the Commons in July 1969 (House of Commons,
1969), of 13 Acts placing duties on local authorities that were
introduced in the parliamentary session 1967—8, only Part II of
the Caravan Sites Act had not been implemented. In passing, it
should be noted that, in arguing for immediate action, Lubbock
continued his integrationist line. He stressed the deprivation of
travellers — 'a section of the community least able to stick up for
itself' — and, in an illuminating passage, made the connection
between education and site provision: 'the educational deprivation
of gypsy children and the consequent impossibility of *fitting
adults into the framework of society* because of limited job opportunities that result from their illiteracy and from the differences

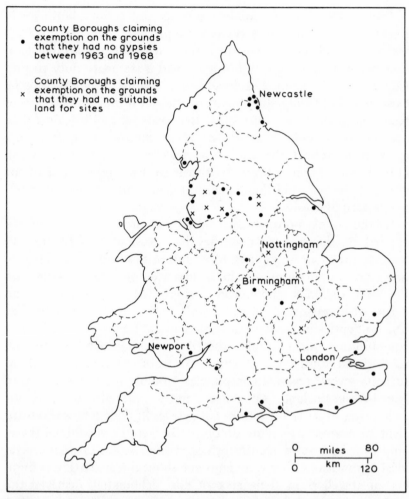

Figure 5   Exemptions claimed under Part II of the Caravan Sites Act, 1968.

between their mores and those of the settled population *will be eliminated* only if we stop hounding them from place to place. ...'
Of more immediate importance was his calculation, based admittedly on limited statistical evidence, that it was costing more for local authorities to evict travellers than it would to provide them with sites. This argument has yet to find acceptance with some city councils.

From 1 April 1970, county councils and county boroughs in England and Wales were obliged to provide sites for travellers residing in and resorting to their areas, with the proviso that London boroughs and county boroughs had a statutory duty to provide only up to 15 pitches. In addition, county boroughs could be exempted from the requirements of the Act if they had no gypsies resorting to their area during the five years up to 1968, or if they had no suitable land available. These limited obligations and exemptions reflect the anti-urban bias of the legislators. Acton (1974) asserts that there was a threat to 'kick gypsies out of the cities altogether', and the exemption clause produced an interesting pattern of evasion.

Of the county boroughs that initially applied for exemption, 12 applied on the grounds that they had no land available and 36 because they had no gypsies. Most authorities in the first category had gypsy populations, and in at least two of these − Dudley, in the West Midlands, and Luton − there had been sustained campaigns of harrassment. Of the county boroughs claiming that they had no gypsies, there were several that had long-established gypsy communities, for example, the Tyneside boroughs, Blackpool, Carlisle and Southampton. The map of non-compliance (figure 5) suggests several regional conspiracies, notably on Tyneside and in North-West England. Of those county boroughs applying for exemption because the number of gypsies in their area was insufficient to warrant provision, 26 out of 36 were successful. Of these, only four have subsequently provided sites. It is clear that several local authorities either were ignorant about the approximate number of travellers in their area or else deliberately deceived the central government.[1] The local strategy of restricting settlement in cities is also suggested by the designation of several county boroughs between 1972 and 1974, that is, the imposition of a ban on travellers beyond those accommodated on the official site. The list of designated boroughs included Leeds, which had one 15-pitch site but over 100 families in the early 1970s, and Wolverhampton,

---

1 Worrall (1979) suggests the latter. He maintains that several local authorities saw the wisdom of making nil returns since it relieved them of the responsibility of providing a site.

which, similarly, had a large traveller population but only one 15-pitch site. After it had been granted designation, Leeds pursued a vigorous policy of eviction. As Worrall (1979) points out, by 1974 there were a total of 46 local authorities that were restricted areas for travellers — gypsies were uniquely discriminated against by the 1968 Act.

CHARACTERISTICS OF SITE LOCATIONS

The slow rate of site development is explained largely by organized opposition to site proposals by house-dwellers. District councillors commonly support the local settled population in its opposition to sites, creating conflict between the county council, which has a statutory obligation to select site locations and construct the sites, and the districts, which respond to local antagonism and often react negatively to site proposals. Cripps argues that 'it is not possible . . . to overstate the intensity of feeling, bordering on the phrenetic, aroused by a proposal to establish a site for gypsies in almost any reasonable location' (Department of the Environment, 1976). As a result, sites are often located in residual areas in order to appease the settled community. The minimization of conflict is a major consideration in the location decision. This means that the environment of sites can be highly undesirable for residential purposes, although, with the constraints on illegal camping in urban areas, the conditions may not be worse than those endured by travellers before they were put on a site. In a survey of 65 sites conducted in 1974, I found that about 28 per cent were located in proximity to industry, either exclusively or in combination with some other use, and 12 per cent were adjacent to land used for waste disposal. The majority of the sites in the sample were situated in agricultural areas, although some of these were also in proximity to industrial or waste disposal uses and only 3 per cent were in residential areas. The picture was one of isolation and/or a polluted environment (see table 1). This pattern of land use associations is also suggested by the Department of the Environment's 1977 register of sites (Department of the

Table 1

Land uses adjacent to permanent sites in England and Wales, 1974

Land use	Number of sites	Percentage of total
Agriculture (incl. forest)	32	49.2
Agriculture/industry	5	7.6
Agriculture/residential	1	1.5
Agriculture/waste disposal	3	4.6
Agriculture/industry/ waste disposal	1	1.5
Industry	13	20.0
Industry/residential	4	6.1
Industry/waste disposal	1	1.5
Waste disposal	1	1.5
Waste disposal/residential	2	3.0
Residential	2	3.0
Totals	65	100.0

Since the definition of adjacent land use was left to the respondent, these figures provide only a rough guide.

Environment, 1977). The following entries seem representative of the less attractive locations.

The triangular site is bounded by high walls on two sides and a high wire fence on the river side and is located in an industrial area. [Dantzig Street, Manchester]

The Oil Street gypsy caravan site has been constructed on the site of the former Waterloo Dock railway goods station. It is located in an industrial/ commercial area. . . . The whole site is enclosed by a substantial brick wall. [Liverpool]

The site is somewhat isolated and there are no residential properties in the immediate vicinity. The site is adjacent to the Grand Union Canal. [Slough, Buckinghamshire]

The site is in an industrial area and is both walled and fenced. [Hull]

The site is situated on an area of former reclaimed swamp bounded on the west by a cotton mill and north by the Leeds and Liverpool canal. [Blackburn]

The site is positioned under the Westway motorway and is bounded on two sides by slip roads and a railway line on the third side. [London, Hammersmith]

Generally, while the object of sites has been to remove trailers from their traditional stopping places where they have been in conflict with the local community, a few have been designed to regularize illegal camps; for example, the Ealing temporary site and the Greenwich permanent site in London, and the Middledyke Lane temporary site on the edge of Hull (closed in May 1980). Experience of the Middledyke Lane site suggests that the establishment of a legal stopping place in itself reduces conflict (see chapter 10), and it is possible that the confirmation of existing patterns of movement in site location planning could, as a principle, satisfy both travellers and the settled community. The problem, however, is to convince hostile house-dwellers of this. The location problem was viewed rather differently by a Joint Working Party of Local Authority Associations and the Gypsy Council, which reported in 1971 (*Caravan Sites Act, 1968, Part II* [n.d.]). It recommended that the locational criteria for conventional residential development, particularly in regard to access to shops, schools and medical facilities, should apply equally to trailer sites. The report departed from the equity principle, however, in suggesting that finding a location quickly was more important than finding one that satisfied the accessibility criteria. In practice, resolution of conflict to the advantage of the settled community has overridden any other locational factors.

SITE DESIGN

The rate of provision and the kinds of location selected for permanent sites have both contributed to disillusionment with the 1968

Act. Travellers spend several years in anticipation of a site; sites are then built in locations that are inconvenient and distant from traditional stopping places; and the provision of a site is used by local authorities as an excuse to harrass and evict those families not accommodated on that site. This sequence of events is not untypical. Problems for travellers are then compounded by the sorts of facilities provided, the layout and the administration of the site.

The range of facilities on the site, their spatial arrangement and the control exercised over their use are interconnected problems that have a bearing on the traveller economy, forms of social behaviour and levels of dissatisfaction. The sort of provision made on a site and the form of management is a problematic issue rather than one where alternative strategies yield clearly definable benefits and costs. It is not simply a case of well equipped sites being better than minimally equipped sites, or vice versa. In theoretical terms, considerations of equity are complicated by the question of freedom and control. Practically, the period during which sites have existed is too short to assess their impact on traveller culture; families on a site react differently to the experience, and it is difficult for a researcher who can make long-term observations on only one or a small number of sites to make sense of the contradictions. Travellers are often unable to express dissatisfaction by leaving a site; other stopping places may be unavailable, or unsatisfactory conditions may be tolerated, for example, because of a family's concern for the continuity of a child's education.

The opposing views on this question are essentially these. The gypsy organizations argue for a high standard of facilities. As Hughie Smith of the National Gypsy Council maintains, there is no reason why travellers should have to accept lower standards of accommodation than the house-dwelling population (*Romano Drom*, the newspaper of the National Gypsy Council, November 1979). In fact, the National Gypsy Council's requirements are modest enough. In response to a Department of the Environment design guide, produced in 1978 without consulting gypsies, the National Gypsy Council recommended that all permanent sites should have electricity, flush toilets and water supply for each trailer; that there should be a warden, preferably a gypsy; that work areas should be provided; and that sites should not accommodate more than 20 trailers. Similarly, Worrall argues for the same standard of facilities as those provided in council housing:

No-one, to the author's knowledge, ever suggested the provision of a 'basic council house' without bathrooms, etc. as a way of cutting costs. To argue for basic sites, therefore, is to argue for discrimination. The minimally equipped site, presented by the government as a form of provision which best fits the lifestyle of many travellers, is a device for withholding resources from travellers. [Worrall, 1979]

What this argument overlooks is that a council that installs expensive facilities on a site is also concerned with protecting its investment. Thus, a tenant is subject to regulations about admissible activities and behaviour that may be severely constraining. On permanent sites there is a general prohibition of fires, which provide a focus for social life on illegal stopping places or unregulated sites; usually, only one dog per family is allowed, and other animals that may have been important economically (such as chickens) or for recreation (like pigeons) are excluded. Further, although some concern was expressed about making provision for scrap-sorting on sites when the Caravan Sites Act was debated in Parliament, many sites do not have any facilities for scrap work, even when located in industrial areas, and we might recall Okely's finding that scrap dealing was less common on permanent sites than on illegal stopping places. If restrictions on economic activity are considered necessary to protect the amenities of a site, then the policing role of the warden assumes greater importance.

A high standard of provision brings with it a spatial order, and this fosters a consciousness of private space which makes it easier to protect the fabric of the site. Boundaries between pitches, between the residential areas and the recreation area (if there is one), between the warden's residence and the rest of the site, and so on, are clearly defined (see figure 1, chapter 4), so that the mixing of categories constitutes a clear violation of the spatial order. This, in turn, emphasizes the role of the warden as a boundary maintainer. To give one example, a family on a site in Hull was threatened with eviction for erecting a storage shed on the space allocated for a garden.

The case for high standards ignores the question of control and constraint from above. While it is reasonable to campaign for the transfer of resources to travellers at the same level as those allocated to council house tenants, since they are all clients of local authorities, it is essential that these resources should be controlled by travellers if they are to retain their autonomy. Traveller control is exceptional, however. Most wardens on sites are *gaujes*, usually social workers; and decisions about the location of a site, the facilities to be provided, and their design are made without consulting the clients. In fact, in a court decision in 1978, Lord Widgery maintained that consultation with gypsies over sites was necessary only in so far as this helped in the acquisition of information required for planning a site. If this information could be acquired elsewhere, there was no need to consult the travellers. This approach to gypsy site development appears to be common practice. While it is not necessarily the case that well-equipped sites are subject to controls that can seriously constrain the economic and social life of the tenants, in practice there is a strong association between the two because the rules for behaviour inevitably reflect the values of the dominant society.

This is a question that fits into a more general debate about social provision, particularly in the field of housing. Turner (1976) has argued forcibly that self-help is a productive strategy for the populations of the *pueblos jovenes* of Peru, and that the lessons drawn from this case in the Third World have more general application. Self-help, he suggests, means that people should not be denied resources but should be given freedom in their utilization − social policy that requires centralized control of resource allocation is misplaced because it denies the capacity of the poor to improve their situation if they are given the resources. As Roberts (1978) suggests in relation to Third World cities, government housing and other social policies are often based on an elitist conception, expressed for example in the idea of a 'culture of poverty'. Change originates from above, and the poor are ineffectual actors in a political and economic sense. The view that they have to be uplifted by a comprehensive social policy 'underestimates the resourcefulness of the poor and the extent to which they participate actively in urban economic and political life'. It is not, then, simply a case of capital and the state reinforcing proletarian status by denying the poor resources representing the antithesis of a policy of allocating resources to the poor through, for example, public housing schemes. The combination of resource allocation and increased control may itself reinforce proletarian status and so the benefits of provision for the poor will be diminished. On the other hand, it must be accepted that self-help can be an empty slogan that legitimates exploitation and neglect. The answer, therefore, would seem to be to release control over resources at the level of the community where there is least likelihood that decisions made on the use of those resources will reflect alien values. In this sense, the analogy between Third World cities and sites for British gypsies is a close one.

RECENT SHIFTS IN GOVERNMENT POLICY

By 1976 the government recognized that Part II of the Caravan Sites Act was a failure. Failure, to the central government, meant that not enough sites had been provided. Accepting a population estimate of from 8,000 to 9,000 families, there was a shortfall of about 300 sites, making no allowance for natural increase, new family formation or immigration. The number of sites built in recent years had been small — 21 in 1974, 15 in 1975, and one in the first 11 months of 1976.

In February 1976, the Minister for Planning and Local Government asked Sir John Cripps to prepare a report on the progress of the Act. This report, *Accommodation for Gypsies,* was critical of local authorities and was immediately dismissed by some councillors. However, it was not as radical as the local authority response might suggest. Cripps maintained that the programme was a failure because the number of sites was grossly inadequate and because the location of many sites was poor from a residential point of view. The locational problem, he recognized, resulted from the identification of incompatible land use associations created by a gypsy site: 'The need for both living and work spaces within the confines of a gypsy site inevitably restrict the choice in planning terms because, in a residential area, they would include a non-conforming use.' This is equally true for an industrial area, but the association with residential areas is one that is politically unacceptable. Of unfavourable locations, Cripps says: 'No non-gypsy family would be expected to live in such places and their unsuitability for gypsies must surely be recognized before long.' Does this imply that councils should close down sites in poor locations, such as badly polluted industrial areas, and relocate them in areas that would be suitable for any residential development?

In accounting for the failure of the Act, Cripps cites three factors. First, there is the hostility of the population where sites are proposed, which has often been extreme. Second, he identifies a number of 'gypsy habits', which seemed to have been gleaned from hearsay rather than any knowledge of traveller culture. Thus, he asserts that

the behaviour of *most* gypsies does nothing to commend them to house-dwellers as neighbours. Indeed, *I have often been told* that they are their own worst enemies; and there is some truth in it ... *they are said to* bully house-dwellers ... those who adopt such methods give the rest a bad name. ... When gypsies are in the neighbourhood, objects disappear from farms and fields and crops are pilfered — *not always* by gypsies, but they are blamed. ... Some families, and especially the children, make themselves objectionable by their insanitary personal behaviour. ...

and so on. This catalogue of deviant behaviour is followed by a suggestion that the problem is associated with illegal stopping places rather than supervised sites, with the clear implication that permanent sites have a useful corrective function. A third factor that Cripps suggests has contributed to the failure of the legislation is the division of responsibility between county and district authorities. As Elcock (1979) remarks, county councillors do not take much of a risk politically if they support the provision of a gypsy site because the area of a county is usually large whereas protests about sites are generally localized. There may be a high political risk for district councillors, however, because they represent small constituencies and most of the electorate could be opposed to a site, which accounts for obstruction and delay at the district level.

Notwithstanding Cripps's misconceptions about traveller culture, and, related to this, his concern for the regulation of their activities, his recommendations required the central government to commit greater resources to the traveller community and to act quickly to comply with the original intention of the 1968 Act. In particular, he recommended 100 per cent central government grants to cover the capital costs of sites, to be available for a five-year period. For those travellers who had the financial means to develop their own sites, he suggested local authority assistance, for example, by giving gypsies first option on land being sold by the council. Thus, finance and land were seen as fundamental in accelerating the rate of site development. It is evident from several local studies, however (see Elcock, 1979, and chapter 10 below), that delay and inaction are due not to lack of money or a shortage of land; the opposition of councillors and residents to site proposals is much more important. In regard to the most suitable size and design of sites, Cripps was clearly uncertain. Small sites, he noted, needed little or no supervision, but proposals for such sites were received with as much hostility as for large sites; large sites were more economical but presented difficulties for supervision. Similarly, he was unsure about the desirable level of facilities. Standards, he argued, have a strong and direct bearing on acceptability and may also affect the cost of supervision, but, while recognizing the advantages of well equipped sites from the local authority's point of view, he saw a case for simple sites where facilities could be upgraded as the need arose. The problem with such honest equivocation is that any local authority could find support for the policy it was pursuing.

Coupled with the requirement to provide sites in the 1968 Act were clauses concerning exemption and designation. As I noted above, a number of cities with established traveller communities had been granted exemption and had, thus, evaded their responsibility. Cripps argued only that local government reorganization in 1974 had created an anomalous situation whereby non-metropolitan counties now contained 18 former county boroughs that had been granted exemption and, since counties could not be exempted, he recommended the cancellation of all exemptions. Designation is a more serious issue. If a local authority is deemed to have made 'adequate provision' and is granted designation, it is then an offence under section 10 of the Act to camp on an unauthorized stopping place and the offender is liable to a fine. In addition, a council can apply to the magistrate's court for a removal order under section 11. Generally, local authorities are anxious to obtain designation once they have provided sites. The County Councils Association has gone farther and suggested the designation of parts of counties as a means of controlling the movements of travellers. This strategy is again inspired by the supposed magnet effect of permanent sites (County Councils Association, 1977). Civil rights groups, such as the National Council for Civil Liberties and the Minority Rights Group, have pointed out that designation discriminates uniquely against travellers since no other ethnic group is restricted in its movements, and the right to a nomadic life, embodied in the Caravan Sites Act, is difficult to reconcile with designation. Migration patterns do not correspond to county boundaries and movements may be occasional and unpredictable. Cripps recognized the difficulties of making sufficient provision and so suggested that designations should be granted only on a county basis and should be subject to a five-yearly review. Rather optimistically, he recommended the provision of temporary stopping places to cater for short-term population increases. What Cripps was apparently unable to accept is that there will be a continuing need to provide sites if designation is introduced and five-yearly reviews will not allow the necessary adjustments in provision to meet demand. Housing programmes are not completed in the way that local authorities envisage gypsy site programmes being completed; the population grows, the housing stock ages, and people need new houses. If it is accepted that travelling is a legitimate alternative to living in a house, the same logic should apply to gypsy site provision.

Finally, Cripps's concern for control, which surfaces at several points in the report, is evident in his recommendations on adminis- tration and management. He suggests the creation of multi-disci- plinary teams of council officers 'to assist gypsies in a variety of matters', and liaison officers to act as go-betweens in negotiations involving local authority agencies and travellers. As Worrall (1979) remarks, 'Where centuries of persecution have failed, bureaucracy might just succeed in the final destruction of the gypsies.'

THE RESPONSE TO CRIPPS

The central government's reaction to Cripps came in Circular 57/78 from the Department of the Environment and the Welsh Office. This document reflected the pressures exerted on the government by local authority associations and there is inevitable dilution in the translation of Cripp's proposals into policy. The Secretaries of State accepted that accommodation for gypsies should be given higher priority, for the benefit of antagonistic house-dwellers as much as for travellers. They agreed to 100 per cent exchequer grants, thus accepting the argument that lack of money was an important factor in the slow rate of site development. Otherwise, they gave some support to the idea of relaxing planning proce- dures but only in vague terms — 'the special need to accommodate gypsies should be taken into account as a material consideration in reaching planning decisions'. The proposal for a gypsy liaison officer in each local authority was endorsed on the grounds that 'he provides an essential link between gypsies and officialdom'. Gypsies, however, could only be co-opted members of council committees or sub-committees. On the site location issue, the circular is equivocal. Thus, reasonable access to services is import- ant, but 'where there is pressure on land suitable for development, proposed gypsy sites may be competing for space with housing and other development' (and so should have a lower priority?). Similarly, polluted environments should be avoided, but 'if a gypsy site includes a work area, giving it something of an industrial character, it may well be inappropriate in close proximity to houses unless the work area is well-screened'. There was, however, an unambiguous recommendation that prospective site tenants should be consulted about suitable facilities and that facilities should be provided in stages — 'the first priority is to establish sites where gypsies may legally camp; the facilities can be up-graded as the need and opportunity occur'. The authors envisage a time when there will be a variety of sites and sites and tenants will have to be matched, so an officer of the local authority will have to assume a gatekeeper role. 'Sites of high quality . . . may be in-appropriate for . . . those unable to accommodate satisfactorily to the stricter regime necessarily prevailing on a well-organized site; the latter may, moreover, prove unacceptable on such sites, both to the management and to the more stable occupants.' This clearly implies an extension of bureaucratic control and it puts the onus on somebody, probably the liaison officer, to discriminate between prospectively 'good' and 'bad' tenants. This could result in the physical separation of families within the same kin group, with socially damaging consequences.

It is clear that the Department of the Environment did not en-visage that designation would limit the freedom of movement of travellers. The circular accepts that the powers given to a local authority by designation are 'severely discriminatory' against one group of people, so it could be granted only where full provision has been made. This recognition of the civil rights of gypsies is difficult to reconcile with their rejection of Cripps's suggestion that designations should be granted only on a county basis, that is, not for smaller areas. The Secretaries of State were 'impressed by the virtual unanimity with which local authorities maintain that provision for designation on a district basis is needed'. The position of the local authorities is hardly surprising, but it is diffi-cult to imagine how district designation could operate without dis-criminating against travellers. Similarly, the suggestion that reviews of designation should be carried out an 'intervals appropriate to local circumstances' is an invitation to local authorities to be parsimonious in providing accommodation.

In summary, the government response to Cripps was less liberal than Cripps, who was not notably liberal in his views himself; in places it was equivocal and so gave local authorities no clear guidelines; and it betrayed the influence of the local authority associations which are primarily concerned with obtaining greater powers to control travellers. None the less, it is possible to discern an advance in thinking since the 1968 Act in that the rights of travellers are given greater recognition; proposals for a greater variety of site designs suggests increased sensitivity to the needs of travellers; and the damaging consequences of some general legislation, such as planning and highways acts, are appreciated.

THE ABORTIVE CARAVAN SITES BILL

The proposals contained in Circular 57/78 were embodied in a new Caravan Sites Bill that was debated in the House of Lords in February 1979 (House of Lords, 1979). This debate was particularly interesting because it involved several people who had contributed to the debates on the 1968 Act, notably Lord Avebury (Eric Lubbock), and the arguments advanced provide a measure of change in attitudes in the light of the Cripps Report and the manifest failure of the original legislation. If anything, positions taken in this debate were more polarized than in the 1960s. Some speakers expressed more radical views than were in evidence in 1968, that is, they were more sympathetic to travellers, but others were as ill-informed and prejudiced as they had been a decade earlier.

The Bill was introduced by Baroness Stedman, who described the problem in essentially the same terms as the Department of the Environment circular. She emphasized the pluralistic basis of policy — 'The majority of gypsies do not want to be anything other than gypsies' — and accepted that travellers were an urban minority. The importance of London as a base for travellers was recognized and the government proposed to repeal all statutory limits for London boroughs. Inner London, the Baroness somewhat grudgingly conceded, should be accessible to travellers and the question of site provision in London should be considered in a regional context. In general, the policy statement, like the earlier circular, was a mixed bag, with concessions both to travellers and to the local authorities reflecting the government's attempt to reconcile conflicting interests.

Baroness Young, for the opposition, supported most of the proposals but betrayed a bias towards the local authority position. Remarkably, she argued that local authorities had made 'a great effort — and it was a great effort — to provide sites', and they had not been given adequate powers to evict illegally parked caravans. So, she was disappointed that the government had not proposed stronger enforcement powers, in addition to district designation. Lord Avebury, in contrast, was highly critical of local authorities — they had failed dismally, and some had skilfully evaded their responsibilities. They had done this, for example, by refusing to participate in a census or by evicting travellers prior to a census and by giving an inflated figure for the number of families accommodated on permanent sites (see chapter 7). He was further critical of local authorities for spending large sums of money on evictions, contrary to central government advice, and he was critical of ministers for being reluctant to use their powers of direction where councils had failed to fulfil their statutory duty. Avebury doubted whether new legislation would be effective because of the determination of some councils to sabotage agreements made between the government and local authority associations. To surmount the problems posed by obstructive local authorities, he was in favour of central direction to facilitate the rapid development of a network of sites — evidently, he had no doubt about the benefits of sites for travellers. In its criticism of government practice, particularly at the local level, this speech was exceptional, and it was not well received by speakers who were averse to central government direction. Further contributions to this debate, however, provided reassurance that attitudes towards gypsies are highly stable, impervious to research findings and to new information, and there was little to provide any hope of a radical alternative to present policy and practice. A few quotations will suffice to indicate the changeless nature of prejudice.

There is a fundamental feeling here, and I wonder if it is not so much the genuine gypsies, the Romany folk, who are under criticism, but the people who go under the banner of gypsies and who are not really gypsies.
... in the Cripps Report one reads that one cannot altogether trust some of these people who come under the heading of gypsies. [Lord Mottistone]

These families go where there are pickings. They do not like to go out into the countryside because they have no affinity with the rural scene. I do not think they are gypsies at all. I believe most of them are scrap dealers who take to the road, perhaps only at certain times of the year. [Lord Gisborough]

I could not agree more that we should let gypsies be gypsies but I would qualify that by saying: let true gypsies be true gypsies. I am sure everybody would want that. [the Earl of Caithness]

... I have come to the conclusion that a great deal of recent legislation has been based on the principle of 'let's find a failure and try to help it, and let's find a success — such as, I suggest, my own industry [agriculture] — and try to ruin it'. Before I beat my sword into a ploughshare I was taught something about reinforcing success and I greatly fear that this Bill may be doing exactly the opposite: namely, reinforcing failure. [Lord Stanley of Alderley]

If we now return to the schematic representation of the problem at the beginning of the chapter, the evidence of parliamentary debates confirms the view that policy is held between the poles of integration and autonomy by liberal forces, concerned with the civil rights of travellers, and by forces concerned with control of the non-conforming aspects of traveller culture, with greater emphasis on the latter. Contradictions in legislative proposals are inevitable because the government has attempted to reconcile opposing attitudes towards travellers. In particular, we find acceptance of the principle of autonomy, which is to be achieved through the construction of a network of sites that will allow both for migration and settlement and allow the continuation of traditional economic activities. However, migrations are largely a response to changing work opportunities, and filling gaps in the market economy depends on a rapid response to the appearance of those gaps. If site provision continues to require negotiation between interested parties at the local level, the development of a network of sites will be slow and patchy, yet district designation

would allow gypsies to migrate freely only if all parts of the network were constructed simultaneously. In short, the pluralist
objective seems idealistic. There is a similar contradiction between
the acceptance of travellers' economic activities and the concern
for standards on sites.

Finally, it is apparent that differences in political philosophy
between parties do not affect thinking on gypsies. All parliamentary debate has been informed by the view that travellers are a
deviant minority that needs to be changed, particularly in its
attitude to land use and employment. The consistency in attitudes
manifested in parliamentary debates since 1967 confirms that
there is a fundamental cleavage between travellers and the rest of
society which is distinct from the class devisions within the dominant system.

CHAPTER 10

Two case studies

Having reviewed individually the cultural attributes of British gypsies and the response of the larger society to certain aspects of their culture, it will be useful to look at the combined effects of the built environment, the local administration and the attitudes of the settled community in particular places. Case studies, because they are holistic but localized in scope, provide a check on bald statements about national or international cultural traits derived from scattered and rather sparse empirical evidence, but we should be aware of some of the limitations of the method.

In regard to the specific problem of travellers' adaptations to the city, data collected for a single urban situation may reflect one of several possible variants of political response while differences in built form and economic activity patterns can also impose variable constraints on the traveller community. One may feel that hypotheses in regard to community conflict — the response of the local administration and so on — are substantiated by observations made in one place, but it would be sensible to retain some scepticism; first, because social and political processes can be manifested in different forms and, second, because the interpretation we put on events depends on our own ideological position. We might be able to speak with greater conviction on the strength of two cases rather than one, and a systematic study of inter-urban variations might represent an advance on a sample of two, but ultimately we have to accept, as Parkin (1979) puts it, that we are using a 'moral vocabulary that reconstructs past and present social reality in an

119

unavoidably slanted way', and no amount of empirical evidence can change this.

It is possible to take some comfort from the fact that the numerous brief reports on the local authority reaction to travellers[1] are remarkably consistent in some respects — for example, assertions about traveller behaviour by councillors are predictable to the point of tedium — but there is evidently some crucial variation in the local authority response in terms of the level of hostility and consistency with central government policy. As Lebas (1977) has noted, there is a particular problem in studying the administration of policy at the local level which stems from the relative autonomy of local government. To some extent, the local state has a life of its own, and thus may oppose central government policy or, at least, be out of step with the centre. Lebas suggests that particular (unspecified) class coalitions in the nineteenth-century may have been institutionalized and have survived as legitimate powers even though their interests may conflict with the interests of the national government, this giving rise to varying interpretations and modes of implementation of central government policies. This is exemplified by the reluctance of some Labour-controlled councils in Britain to implement public expenditure cuts. The relevance of this argument is suggested in the following accounts of the response to travellers in Hull and Sheffield, particularly in regard to their interpretation of the 1968 Caravan Sites Act and their compliance with the central government's advice on the treatment of travellers pending the provision of permanent sites.

Hull and Sheffield were not selected for study after a careful consideration of alternatives. Rather, the choice of Hull was dictated by my own experience with travellers there and with local authority officers and councillors, while Sheffield is a city where the treatment of gypsies by the local authority has been given prominence in the regional and national press — the seriousness of the conflict there suggests that the problem may contain

---

1 See, for example, reports in *Traveller Education*, Walsall, and in *Romano Drum*, the newspaper of the National Gypsy Council.

ingredients that are missing in Hull. The information on which these accounts are based is derived from personal observation and reports in local newspapers.[2] The latter are invariably biased, but should not be dismissed as a source of data on that account. Comments by councillors, which provide an important clue to policy, are generally reported verbatim while, otherwise, it is possible to distinguish the factual from the mythical by checking against other sources of information.

HULL

During the past decade, there have been from 60 to 80 travelling families using Hull either as a permanent or a temporary base. Nearly all local families have forsaken seasonal migrations into the surrounding countryside in recent years and now live permanently in the city, but there is a social network that extends to other towns, particularly York, Thorne (near Doncaster) and Gainsborough, Lincolnshire. As I suggested in chapter 8, the association with Hull is probably a long one.

This group of local families is quite distinct from the smaller element of long-distance, mostly Irish, travellers, who stay for a few weeks at a time, usually in the summer although a few long-distance travellers have spent the winter in the city. These travellers are distinct from the local families in the sense that there is little, if any, social interaction between the two groups and their economic interests differ. For the long-distance traveller, Hull provides a market for tarmacing and is a good source of antique furniture, which is sold in other parts of the country where prices are higher. The local travellers have a number of sources of income. There is not enough manufacturing activity in the region to generate the quantity of scrap that could support travellers as full-time scrap dealers, and hawking and farmwork are important complementary occupations. None of this work is particularly lucrative,

---

2 The newspapers consulted were the *Hull Daily Mail* and, in Sheffield, *The Morning Telegraph* and *Star*.

however, and most local families are poor by traveller standards. In the early 1970s, Hull's travellers were conspicuously poorer than most, many living in wagons or cheap trailers, with the children dressed traditionally and largely in second-hand clothes. They have subsequently modernized in a superficial sense as a result of living permanently in the city, where involvement with institutions, such as schools, and the use of public houses and working men's clubs encourages some surface conformity. Youth culture, for example, cuts across the gypsy–*gauje* boundary, and several young gypsy men have been involved in the Teddy Boy revival. However, this sort of interaction with the larger society is possible for individuals or small groups only in situations where ethnic identity is of little or no consequence – the traveller community as a whole is still strongly bounded, geographically and socially.

The city

The possibilities offered by a city for settlement and economic exploitation are related to the form of ownership and the management of land and buildings. This is important in two respects: first, in regard to the creation and elimination of marginal space, and, second, in regard to the reaction of the settled community to outsiders. The latter connection is an indirect one; cities in which the local authority has a large role in housing the population are characterized by residential areas that are, in Mary Douglas's terms, particularly susceptible to threat and violation, both because of their location (peripheral estates) and because of their social and physical homogeneity. In Hull the local authority is the principal provider of houses. Over 90 per cent of new housing built between 1948 and the early 1970s has been constructed for local authority tenants, while the city council sees its housing problem as worse than that of many other British cities and, as a result, has an extensive clearance programme. Most of the new residential development in the early 1960s and early 1970s was in the form of peripheral estates, with a subsequent shift of emphasis to inner-city renewal. In spite of the possibilities created by the

1969 and 1974 Housing Acts, rehabilitation has occurred on only a small scale, with one General Improvement Area, involving 600 dwellings.

The singular emphasis on renewal in the current housing strategy suggests that much of the nineteenth-century housing stock has been written off, but this policy has given rise to very little conflict between the local authority and residents.[3] This lack of protest, which Dunleavy (1977) has recognized as a salient feature of relationships between local authorities and low-income groups, probably indicates that most of the working class see themselves solely as clients of the council in the acquisition of housing, and accept, albeit reluctantly, the constraints and regulation that are associated with local authority tenancy. Realistically, they appreciate that other options are not available to them. Physically, the local authority dominance of housing has resulted in a characteristic mixture of high-rise flats and terraces on peripheral estates and the monotonous repetition of a two-storey terrace design in the inner city — what was formerly a large area of nineteenth-century terrace housing is shrinking rapidly. This has important consequences for the gypsy community.

First, there are immediate opportunities for stopping in the older residential areas as a result of the numbers of derelict houses and their eventual clearance. Most of the stopping places in the inner city shown in figure 6 are of this type. This allows travellers to continue an association with a part of the city where, in the past, they have lived in houses or stopped in yards at the rear of houses. Further, the inclusion of an area in a compulsory purchase order depresses the prices of old property, and several gypsy families have thus been able to buy or rent short-life houses very cheaply. Most families in the inner city, however, are on the road and move about as the abandonment and demolition of houses creates new stopping places. In the next few years, however, it is probable that the whole of the inner-city zone presently constitut-

---

3 In two isolated instances of public inquiries into renewal schemes where residents organized opposition to the council's proposals and campaigned for Housing Action Area status, the Secretary of State for the Environment ruled in favour of the council.

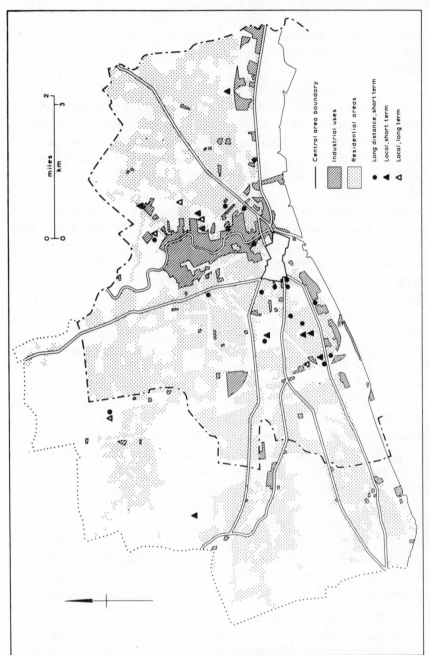

Figure 6   The location of stopping places in Hull, 1970—9.

ing the travellers' territory will be redeveloped, thereby eliminating opportunities for adaptation to this kind of urban change. Importantly, at the moment the city council tolerates illegal occupation of cleared sites.

The other consequence of local authority housing programmes for the settlement of gypsies in the urban area has been that the boundary between travellers and council tenants on the edge of the city has been sharply defined. In effect, this means that the tenants have a heightened perception of the order and homogeneity of the estate environment, which is contrasted with the disorder of travellers' camps on adjacent roadsides and fields. The principal conflict zone in the 1970s has been along this boundary, where the travellers' traditional stopping place is now in close proximity to the perversely named Orchard Park estate, built during the 1960s. This conflict has been the central issue in authority—traveller relations and has affected all aspects of policy.

The council's role as developer and landowner has also been significant on the outer edge of the industrial zone of the city, along the River Hull, where land is held in reserve for further factory development. This land has provided extensive free grazing for the traveller's horses and has been used as an alternative stopping place to the main sites on the north-western edge of the city. Conflict here has been with the council's Department of Industrial Development, which considers that the presence of travellers on council land detracts from the image it wishes to present to potential investors. This zone contrasts with the older industrial area, closer to the city centre, where travellers have stopped on derelict land with little harrassment. As with the residential areas of the city, there are variations in sensitivity related to the political and economic significance of particular zones in the development strategy for the city.

So far, this account has dealt only with areas where the local authority is the landowner or has a major interest in land and property, as in the inner city. This is because travellers have customarily stopped in such areas; conflict between gypsies and the residents of privately developed estates has been insignificant, not because the residents are tolerant, but because few travellers

have camped near middle-class suburbs. Protests following proposals to develop official sites near high-status areas clearly indicate that social class and tenure category of residents are unrelated
to the level of hostility towards travellers, although there *is* an
apparent difference between the suburban fringe, where residents
are concerned with maintaining social distance between themselves
and other groups, or where the political interests of the council
coincide with the political allegiances of the residents (in the case
of Orchard Park, predominantly Labour voters, which a Labour
council does not wish to alienate), and the inner city. In the latter
zone, the social composition of the population, the forms of
tenure, the condition of the housing stock and the generally seedy
environment do not appear to provide the conditions for conflict
between *gaujes* and travellers. The two groups have some shared
economic interests, particularly in the rag and bone trade ('tat-
ting'); many residents will be anticipating a move to a new house
and so will be less likely to defend their neighbourhood against
outsiders; and, in a zone of mixed uses and disuse, travellers do
not constitute visible pollution in the sense that they do on a
strongly classified peripheral estate.

The recent history of conflict

In the 1960s, local travellers in the Hull area had a number of
stopping places on the urban fringe which were used for short
periods; evictions were frequent and are recalled with an air of
resignation. The police would tell families to move on 'to give the
grass a chance to grow again', and there was little resistance from
the travellers. At this time, the boundary between the older
council estate in North Hull and the agricultural land to the west
was recognizable as a point of conflict. Thus, in April 1965
travellers who were stopping on land close to the estate met
opposition from residents, who put pressure on the council to
evict them. Initially they were identified not as gypsies in the local
press but as 'caravan dwellers', conveying the impression that they
were of obscure identity and unknown origin. The first newspaper

report was quite restrained but a subsequent one was bizarre. With the headline 'Night horsemen shatter the peace', it asserted that 'the night was shattered by the galloping hooves of the gypsies' horses up and down a street of a Hull Corporation estate', and the article contained other unsubstantiated accusations of deviancy, including the theft of meat and milk from houses. The council reaction was largely negative. The chairman of the town planning committee, for example, commented that 'The only way we can deal with them is to show them that we don't want them in the city. I understand that Leeds had a clear-out a few months ago, and we are satisfied that a good many of those who were in the city centre came from other towns.' One councillor, however, did suggest that site provision was the only sensible answer to the problem.

By 1970 the Caravan Sites Act of 1968 had become effective, and the Gypsy Council was providing a focus for political organization at the national level and was getting involved in some local disputes. There was little evidence of political awareness among travellers in Hull at this time, but they became much more conscious of the possibilities for resistance in the next few years. At the end of 1970 most families had returned to Hull for the winter and had stopped on land near the Orchard Park estate, provoking the customary hostility from estate residents and extensive press coverage, with reference to 'hundreds of gypsies' and an eviction threat by Hull Corporation. This was withdrawn after a newly formed travellers' support group had protested to the council, but the threat of eviction was enough to make some families move to other stopping places in the urban area.

This confrontation, the 1968 Act and pressure from the Gypsy Council and the local support group together prompted the local authorities involved – East Riding County Council, Hull Corporation and Haltemprice Council, which administered Hull's western suburbs and the adjacent rural area – to make a positive response. They began a search for permanent sites, and in March 1971 the health committee of Haltemprice council produced a list of six possible sites, one of which was Middledyke Lane, Cottingham, the main traditional stopping place near the Orchard Park estate.

Their concern was manifestly with integration and control. As one councillor commented, they had a duty to accommodate the gypsies and educate them to tidiness, while another asserted that 'while I have every sympathy with them, they should be made to toe the line'. Meanwhile, the conflict between the Orchard Park tenants and the travellers continued and became more acute. In October 1972 an anti-gypsy action group, with the support of two Labour councillors, sent a petition to Hull council, demanding eviction of the travellers from Middledyke Lane, a demand Hull was unable to meet since the travellers were camped by the roadside and could be evicted only by the county council under the 1959 Highways Act. (The responsibility of various councils was complicated by the fact that the land used by travellers, when not on the roadside, was owned by Hull Corporation but administered by Haltemprice Council.) Any move against the travellers in Middledyke Lane was, in any case, deferred pending an inquiry into a proposal for a permanent site in the village of Dunswell, north of Hull.

The Dunswell proposal met strong opposition from local residents, who, apart from voicing the usual objections to gypsies, cited the danger of infection for brucellosis-free pedigree cattle. The convenient argument that a gypsy site was an industrial use and, therefore, out of place in a rural area was used several times by objectors, but the travellers also had reservations about the site. They were worried about its remoteness and the danger to children from deep drainage ditches and a nearby river. This left only the county council supporting the proposal and, following a public inquiry in August 1973, the application was rejected.

The Orchard Park conflict now became more acute. There was a further petition to Hull council and meetings of the anti-gypsy action group at which accusations of deviancy were quite unrestrained. At one meeting, for example, a Conservative alderman said: 'I have taken a tour of the area and I will not beat about the bush. Any self-respecting person would take a detour. The whole area is quite deplorable.' Recalling a visit to a former site in an industrial area of Hull, which was not designed for travellers, she said: 'I have never been so horrified to see the rubbish, the filth and damage, with toilets smashed and basins pulled from the walls.' This protest culminated in a demonstration of placard-waving tenants on the boundary of the estate, facing the travellers stopping place, in August 1973 ('How much longer do we have to put up with this shanty town on our estate?'; 'Smokeless zone — gypsies burn car tyres, we would be fined'; 'Give a thought to tenants who suffer harrassment' [*sic*], and so on) — an event largely ignored by the gypsies. The issue was kept on the boil by the announcement of the government's rejection of the Dunswell site in December 1973, and by the occupation of a field in Hull's green belt by several traveller families in January 1974. This occupation was arranged by Hughie Smith, of the National Gypsy Council, in order to put pressure on Hull Corporation to provide an official site. The city council acted quickly by serving an eviction notice and then establishing a site without planning permission on Middledyke Lane, denying that the occupation of green belt land had anything to do with their decision. Their move was endorsed by the county council; the Orchard Park tenants expressed outrage, and Haltemprice council, as planning authority, objected, but Hull went ahead with the development. A further event in April 1974 sustained the conflict. A group of about 12 long-distance Irish travelling families moved on to land adjacent to the new temporary site at Middledyke Lane for what would be, inevitably, a short stay. Since the city council was sensitive about the site issue, it immediately served eviction notices on the families and they left soon after for a stopping place in the inner city. In the light of events during the preceding months, this rather unimportant event was seen by some council members and officers and by the Orchard Park tenants as something that would increase tension and hostility, and the issue was greatly amplified by the local newspaper, which gave its reports larger headlines than any previous gypsy news. The first report, headed, 'Crisis talks as gypsies rush to North Hull site', began, 'North Hull's gypsy crisis flared up again today when dozens of caravan families were reported heading for the Middledyke Lane site', and later the paper reported 'an eleventh hour bid to avert an ugly confrontation'.

The following month, following local government reorganization, Beverley Borough Council, which succeeded Haltemprice
council as the district authority, served an enforcement notice on
Hull city council, requiring it to close down the Middledyke Lane
site. Hull appealed against the order, a public inquiry was held,
and the Secretary of State for the Environment ruled in favour of
Beverley council but gave Hull two years to clear the site, a dead-
line that has been extended several times. Subsequently, small
improvements were made to the minimally equipped site, containment of the travellers was achieved by ploughing the 200 metres
of land between the site and the estate, and Middledyke Lane
failed to generate further political excitement.

During the same period, from 1970 to 1975, a small number of
local travellers stopped on council land reserved for industry, part
of which was near a new suburban housing development. There
were repeated eviction attempts, sometimes initiated by the
council and sometimes in response to complaints from local residents, but these were resisted with some success by travellers and
the local support group by arguing that the children's education
would be interrupted, or, if this failed, by moving a short distance
to land not included in the possession order. Increasingly, the
provision of education and the involvement of the social services
with the travellers were used as arguments against eviction, and the
local authorities were eventually convinced of this, evidently
because the acceptance of the welfare agencies by the travellers
suggested an increasing integration into the larger society. The
County Planning Officer, for example, spoke in 1977 of the
importance of maintaining 'these fragile links' with the travellers
in advising the district authorities not to harass them. None the
less, the occupation of the council's industrial land was held to be
intolerable, and there was a final eviction in 1975. The council
panicked when about 15 long-distance Irish families moved on to
a field occupied by six local families, who had been left alone for
several months. The council's perception of the Irish arrival as an
invasion (and the officials' poor arithmetic) is indicated in the following extract from evidence given to the county court in an
application for the possession of the land (under Order 26, King-
ston-upon-Hull County Court, 19 July 1975):

At the time of service of the said Notice I did identify the persons named as respondents but was unable to identify other persons who were in occupation as, at the time of service, the land was occupied by 39 or more caravan dwellings. This number *was increasing by the hour* and I formed the opinion that identification of all the occupants would be impossible. [my emphasis]

Following this eviction, an extensive earthwork was erected to discourage further invasions.

While the city council was exercised in placating its tenants and protecting its land holdings on the urban fringe, it was less concerned with the removal of travellers from the inner city, even though there were, on occasions, as many families stopping near the city centre as there were on the edge of the city. The inner-city gypsies are both long-distance travellers who stop on any vacant site for a few weeks and local travellers who try to establish a niche in the older residential areas. Travellers have been subject to eviction in this part of the city but there has been little or no hostility from the local house-dwellers, for reasons I have suggested above. Also, few conflicts between the travellers and authority have gone as far as the council applying for a possession order, and there has been little publicity.

Exceptionally, the eviction of a group of both local and long-distance travellers camped on land on the edge of the central area in 1965 was given sensational coverage in the local newspaper — 'Caravan squatters told "Out you go"'; 'Hull gets tough with fifty families'. As in other reports at this time, there was no recognition that the families were gypsies, and they were portrayed as if they existed in a cultural vacuum. The sort of adaptations they had made in the area, however, indicated that they were probably local travellers. For example, one traveller was using a derelict industrial building as a workshop, and others were breaking up scrap metal in abandoned houses. The chairman of the city planning committee maintained that 'we have to start to be tough with them', and the council took the unusual and ineffective step of advertising the notice of eviction in the local newspaper rather than serving eviction notices on individual families. From the reported comments of travellers, it is apparent that several had spent the winter in the city and one had been stopping in a street in his trailer with mains electricity supply for 14 years.

Since the mid-1970s, the council has been clearing and re-
developing working-class housing in the western part of the inner
city (the Hessle Road area), a process that has yielded an extensive
stock of empty houses, left standing for up to a year, and cleared
sites. As the clearance has progressed from west to east, local
travellers have occupied the empty spaces and have used the
vacant houses as stables and workshops, moving on as the land is
taken for redevelopment. Other families have rented short-life
properties, but some of these have gone back on the road after a
few years in the house. The long-distance travellers have also taken
advantage of the opportunities for stopping created by the clearance programme but have tended to move on to any marginal land
that might provide short-term security, such as railway land next
to the station and a space behind a supermarket in a major shopping street. Travellers find the inner city attractive because of the
supply of free land and buildings, proximity to shops and schools,
kinship ties in the area and the tolerance of local residents. Given
the scale of the clearance schemes, opportunities for stopping in
the inner city will exist for several years yet, but it is likely that
this association with the inner city will no longer be possible when
redevelopment is completed and the unfinished environment is
transformed to a clearly bounded one. The travellers will then
emerge as a conspicuously non-conforming element, and the only
officially accepted equation will be between travellers and permanent sites. Against this, we might argue that travellers have
demonstrated their ability to seek out marginal space, and it is a
real possibility that Hull's housing programme will never eliminate
decay and dereliction and the need for clearance. Thus, the supply
of stopping places may allow continuing residence in the inner city
in the long term.

Permanent sites

Before local government reorganization in 1974, Hull Corporation
and the East Riding County Council conducted a search for possible site locations, the result of which is shown in figure 7. The

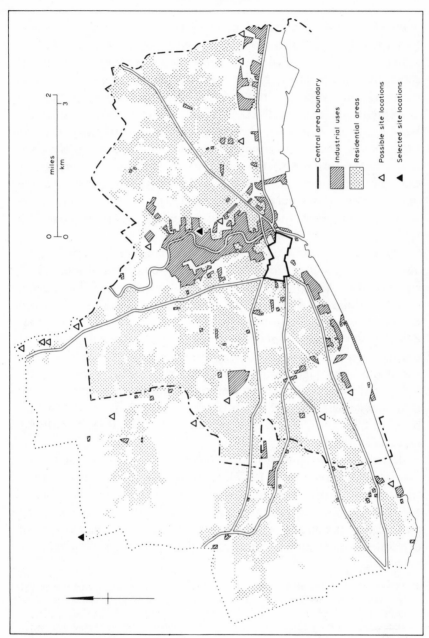

Central area boundary

Industrial uses

Residential areas

△ Possible site locations

▲ Selected site locations

Figure 7   Site locations in Hull proposed by the former East Riding County Council and Hull Corporation.

map reflects the importance attached to the minimization of conflict with the residential population, with most locations being in
either rural or industrial areas. Only two were within residential
areas, but three out of the 17 were stopping places on the urban
fringe already used by travellers. Thus, the existing pattern of
movement made a small contribution to the planning strategy.
Most locations were then eliminated, including Middledyke Lane,
Cottingham, because of a pledge by Labour members of Humberside County Council to the residents of the Orchard Park estate
that this temporary site would not be upgraded to a permanent
one.[4] (Privately, several councillors and officers conceded that this
would be the best site from the travellers' point of view, but
politically it was impossible.)

The two locations that the county council recommended to the
district councils in 1975 were the most remote rural location —
Harland Way, Cottingham, in Beverley borough, and Wilmington
railway sidings, in Hull's major industrial area. Hull city council
accepted the Wilmington proposal on the understanding that
Beverley would simultaneously develop the Harland Way site, but
the reaction of the rural authority was largely hostile. It should be
noted that, although groups supporting the travellers were consulted, the travellers themselves were not involved in policy formulation, notwithstanding the fundamental impact that sites would
have on their lives. There is, however, nothing unusual in planning
on behalf of travellers.

Although development of the Wilmington site proceeded quite
rapidly (it was opened in 1977), there were objections from industrialists who had plants adjacent to the site. Thus, one member of
the Hull Chamber of Commerce claimed that the decision was 'the
thin edge of the wedge — just when the industrialists had got rid of
delinquents and vandals continually damaging their property, the

---

4   Elcock (1979) describes this site as 'highly unsatisfactory', but the travel-
    lers considered its location to be a good one. Also, although its physical
    condition was poor, it did provide free living space without the regulation
    and constraint characteristic of permanent sites. There is evidently much
    greater dissatisfaction with the rural site to which some of these families
    were moved.

council had brought in this potential danger'. Again, a gypsy site was seen as non-conforming, even though an earlier justification for this particular location put forward by the county council had been that gypsies are scrap dealers, and therefore should live in industrial areas. All housing in the area is being cleared on the grounds that it is an unsuitable residential environment, but the lack of separation of residence and workplace invariably works to the disadvantage of travellers when they are categorized by the planning authority. The land used for the site is surrounded by manufacturing industry and waste tips, and there is serious air pollution, with one chemical plant making low-level emissions from a chimney less than 100 metres from the site. The initial reaction of the travellers who were allocated places was favourable, which was not surprising since most of the families had moved from Middledyke Lane, which was very muddy and lacking in basic facilities and now they had hard standings, concrete roadways, hot and cold water and lavatories. The local newspaper was ecstatic 'the grass is springing up and the 24 families living there look out onto the beautiful flowers and rock gardens which they have put in — and the site itself is beginning to bloom'. In fact, one traveller had started a garden on his plot — otherwise, there were few indications of the adoption of the *gauje* life-style. In the two-and-a-half years since the site has opened, dissatisfaction has increased. Particular concern is expressed about air pollution, which travellers associate with headaches and bronchial troubles, high rents, the lack of control over other families' dogs, and too much control — for example, the prohibition of additonal sheds under the site rules. Although the warden is tolerated as an individual, there have been adverse comments about his/her role, both because he/she does too little and does too much. This ambivalence seems to reflect a general resentment of supervision by an outsider, and I find this impossible to reconcile with Elcock's (1979) endorsement of site wardens: 'the provision of wardens is crucial if vandalism and nuisance are to be prevented and their usefulness as a channel of communication between gypsies and the local authorities is very considerable' (thus denying the travellers' capacity to communicate their needs themselves).

A further shortcoming of the site, which applies to sites in general, is the constraint it imposes on interaction within extended families. This is reflected in the practice of families related to those living on the site stopping illegally beyond the perimeter fence in order to maintain close physical proximity — for example, a woman who wishes to keep in close contact with her mother during pregnancy. Finally, although scrap dealing was advanced as an occupational characteristic that influenced the choice of location, there are no facilities for scrap sorting or storage. During 1979 several families moved off, preferring to stop illegally and without facilities in the clearance areas in the inner city, but dissatisfaction is not yet reflected in the level of occupation of the site owing to the general shortage of stopping places in the city. It is clear, however, that the site location and design are poor from the user's point of view and the development is successful only in the context of local politics — the council has fulfilled part of its obligation under the 1968 Caravan Sites Act with little hostility from the house-dwelling majority.

The development of the Harland Way site has proceeded much less smoothly. Although both Hull and Beverley councils had agreed in 1975 to provide one site each, Beverley went back on its agreement in 1976, following the district council elections in which the Conservatives gained control. The decision not to build the site, supported by 34 votes to 13, was justified by arguments that carried little conviction — the site would present a danger to livestock; there was inadequate grazing for the travellers' horses, which would each require an acre of land; the location was too remote for the travellers; and so on. A more likely reason for rejection was that the residents of suburban Cottingham, in which the site would be located, were vehemently opposed to it, and many of the councillors shared their prejudice. Notwithstanding the information on the problem provided by the county planning department, the stereotypes were retained. One district councillor, who was a member of the county planning committee, commented in familiar fashion: 'These people should not be allowed to live rent and rates free. They are not gypsies. They are travelling businessmen. They should be like everyone else and have to find their own premises and pay rates and rent.' Hull's development and estates committee condemned Beverley's decision, and the county planning department refused to reopen the issue of site location. However, as Elcock (1979) relates, Beverley persisted in its approach and asked the Secretary of State for the Environment to re-examine the planning application. This it refused to do, but the owner of the site then forced the county council to purchase the land compulsorily, causing further delay. The compulsory purchase order was confirmed in January 1978, but the council then delayed site construction until it was able to apply for a 100 per cent central government grant.[5] The site was opened in 1980, five years after the original planning application. Thus, ten years after the 1968 Caravan Sites Act became effective, travellers in the Hull area have two permanent sites, accommodating about two-thirds of the local population and no long-distance travellers. If additional space is not provided, the proportion of the population with legal accommodation will decline as a result of new family formation and a high rate of natural increase. There is, therefore, no case for designation.

The Hull study demonstrates several features of the relationship between travellers and the dominant society in an urban area, which may have wider application. The marginal space utilized by travellers is localized, in the inner city and on the urban fringe. The reaction to this use by the larger society varies according to the perceived threat presented by the presence of travellers, but there is in Hull a fairly consistent difference between a weakly classified (inner-city) and a strongly classified (suburban) environment. Of particular interest in relation to theories of community conflict is the alliance of working-class Labour voters and Labour councillors on peripheral estates against the travellers, which may be taken as evidence that there is a basic social cleavage between the dominant society and the minority, with travellers divided from the working-class majority by a firm cultural boundary. In

---

5 This followed a recommendation by Cripps, in his report *Accommodation for Gypsies* (Department of the Environment, 1976), that the central government should finance the construction of sites to speed up provision.

relation to site provision, inter-authority conflict along party lines at the district level is clearly important in accounting for the lack of progress, as is the relative impotence of the county council and the central government: the intransigence of Beverley council demonstrates a degree of district level autonomy. Eventually, central government policy may be implemented, but the district council's capacity to obstruct and delay is considerable. In the local government system, it is only the district councillor whose political success depends on responding to local prejudice and who faithfully reflects grass-roots antagonism — which 'liberal' central government policy attempts to override.[6] The lack of common ground between different levels of government on the gypsy site issue is analogous to the problem described by Reyner Banham in his account of a public participation exercise carried out by city planners in Los Angeles (cited by Ward, 1976). When asked by participants, 'How can I get the Mexicans out of my neighbourhood?' they realized that officials and the public had rather different conceptions of planning problems. Finally, it is notable that little of this political conflict has involved the travellers directly. Many decisions made on their behalf are learned indirectly, usually by rumour, and the reaction to news about sites and other policy affecting them often appears to be one of resignation or indifference.

SHEFFIELD

The Labour-controlled city council in Sheffield has a reputation for generous provision of services, for example, in the fields of housing and education, and the allegedly excessive level of spend-

---

6 Two comments are relevant. Elcock (1979) asks 'whether intellectuals and professional people have the right to foist sites on others despite their wishes'. Similarly, Parkin (1979) suggests that there is an element of class conflict in liberal social policy that is manifest in the 'accusation by workers and the "respectable poor" that they are expected to bear the entire social costs of minority group incorporation because the middle-class advocates of reform are carefully shielded from the social impact of their own recommendations'.

ing is a major point of contention for the Conservative opposition on the council. Included in the education programme is special provision for the teaching of racial and ethnic minorities, and in 1979 the education committee advertised for a teacher to be concerned specifically with the development of a multi-cultural curriculum and the fostering of links with the (white) community in schools in the east end of Sheffield, where the Asian community is concentrated. This area — Tinsley, Attercliffe and Darnall — is also the part of Sheffield occupied by the travellers. They have a long association with the eastern industrial zone of the city, which is dominated by steel works, steel fabricating plants and scrap yards. Housing dates mostly from the late nineteenth-century and is now being cleared, with some new development on the outer edge of the area, while the inner area is zoned for industry. With the decay and clearance of the older residential property, commercial activities along Attercliffe Road are experiencing a parallel decline, with a large number of dilapidated structures, vacant premises and a predominance of low-threshold functions, such as second-hand shops. It is, in other words, a typical declining inner-city area where the local authority's policies characteristically involve clearance, partial renewal of housing and single-use zoning to eliminate the mixture of housing and heavy industry.

From newspaper reports of conflicts and from personal surveys, it is evident that the area of Sheffield habitually occupied by travellers is very small (figure 8). There is an obvious economic link with the east end, namely, that most families are involved in scrap dealing and proximity to scrap yards and the steel mills minimizes transport costs, but this part of the city also constitutes the social space of the gypsy community. A gypsy woman born in Darnall in 1900 recalls how the travellers kept their wagons in the yards of public houses in the district early in the century, and the association persists. It is notable that travellers evicted from illegal stopping places have generally moved only short distances, keeping contact with their familiar territory, and this pattern of behaviour supports the view that local travellers in British cities are largely sedentary, having close links, in particular, with older working-class areas. This highly localized pattern of traveller occupation is

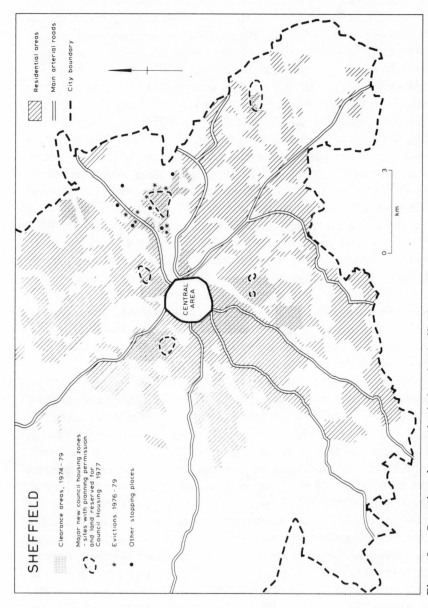

SHEFFIELD

Clearance areas, 1974–79

Major new council housing zones
– sites with planning permission
and land reserved for
Council Housing 1977

* Evictions 1976–79

• Other stopping places

CENTRAL
AREA

Residential areas

Main arterial roads

City boundary

0   km   3

Figure 8   Stopping places and evictions in Sheffield, 1976–9.

important politically, since the area they occupy is a traditional source of Labour support and also because much of the population of Sheffield will be aware of travellers only through information provided by the media — commuting to the city centre from most directions does not involve passing gypsy trailers. This means that local newspapers have an important role in interpreting conflicts between travellers and house-dwellers and in informing the popular response. Consequently, we need to assess the contribution of the local press to deviancy amplification.

The official response

Conflict between travellers and the local authority in Sheffield has been episodic, with two periods of intense activity by the council, designed to exclude gypsies from the city, in 1968 and 1969 and from 1976 to 1981. This negative reaction has been complemented by a search for sites which has been a source of political conflict along party lines in the council.

About 30 local travelling families spent the winter of 1967—8 camped in a disused greyhound stadium in Darnall. They were evicted in March 1968, moved to waste land about half a mile away, were again evicted following a petition to the city council from local residents and a march by Attercliffe housewives to the town hall; then followed two more forced moves, all within the same area. A spokesman for Sheffield corporation asserted that the city had been 'lightly affected' before this period so that there had been no need to consider the construction of a permanent site. The local authority was not accommodating. The town clerk, for example, maintained that 'one can never make promises to trespassers. They claim the right to go on private land. It's the usual thing, something for nothing.' There were the customary accusations of deviancy, including one from a Darnall councillor at a city council meeting: 'Members gasped in amazement when he said, "Six of the gypsies went into one of the public houses. They drank eight dozen bottles of stout in 20 minutes but the landlord barred them after that".' The travellers were also attributed with

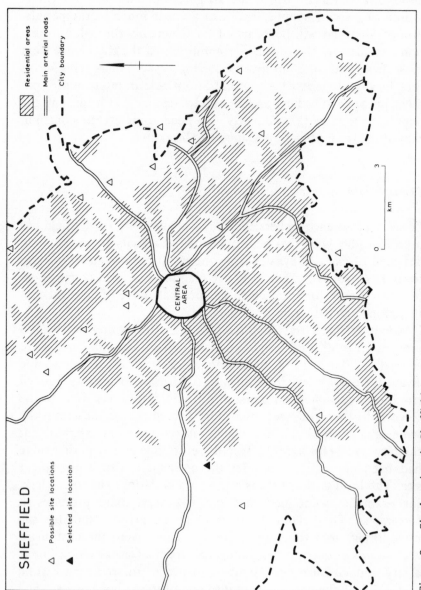

Figure 9   Site locations in Sheffield proposed by the city council.

an unlikely preference for nude bathing in the boating lake in the local park.

Although the council was more concerned at this time with meeting the demands of hostile residents than with making provision for travellers, a search for sites was initiated, partly as a result of pressure from the Gypsy Council. As figure 9 indicates, the locations proposed as possible sites had a peripheral pattern, similar to the pattern emerging from Hull's search, but otherwise there is no marked spatial bias. However, of the possible locations, three were close to the Attercliffe—Darnall area. When the number of options was narrowed down a clear political split emerged over a desirable location. The controlling Conservative group suggested a site at Handsworth, in the industrial south-east, which was opposed by Labour councillors on the grounds that this proposal was designed to keep gypsies away from Conservative voters. The council then opted for a site for 15 trailers at Tinsley Locks, in Attercliffe, on land flanked by a factory, a railway and allotments, and close to a canal. This decision was also opposed by the Labour group, who argued, not entirely convincingly, that it was unsuitable for the travellers and, more to the point, that it was too close to residential areas populated by Labour voters. As a Labour alderman put it: 'If the gypsies are to be given a chance to conform and if they intend to conform, they have to be isolated. That is an absolute must. They cannot be taught to conform where they are, living in the kind of area they have been up to now.' There was a public inquiry in November 1968, and the proposal was rejected. In 1969 a new list of possible sites was drawn up, with some locations retained from the earlier proposals (the combined lists are mapped in figure 9). This strategy was criticized by a Labour councillor for spatial bias, since ten out of the 16 locations were on the east side of the city. This, he asserted, was unfair, and he recommended that 'these people should have a rural setting'. Meanwhile, evictions continued, but the occupation of one officially sanctioned stopping place in Darnall was maintained until its final abandonment by travellers in 1978 and its subsequent closure by the council, removing the only place from which there was not an immediate risk of eviction.

The problem resurfaced in 1976. The Labour group had re-
gained control of the city council and their proposal was to develop
a site on a former prisoner-of-war camp at Redmires, on the west
side of the city, a location that was on the original list of alternatives. This suggestion generated a debate identical to that over the
earlier plan for a site on the east side, but with the roles reversed.
Both Labour and Conservative councillors were explicit in their
arguments about the political basis of the decision. Thus, a Labour
member declared that 'it was unfair to expect the people of Attercliffe and Darnall to bear the gypsy problem alone', and a Conservative councillor objected that 'Lodge Moor people [the western
suburb in which Redmires is located] could be forgiven for thinking that there is a feeling of malice in the city council's decision.
There are not many Labour supporters in the area'. Later, Councillor Wilson, the leader of the Labour group who has made
several highly prejudiced statements about travellers, said that 'it
is about time that we got them out of the hair of the people of the
east end'. Similarly, the council leader, Sir Ron Iremonger, maintained that Redmires was the ideal site 'If they [the Tories]
wanted them [the travellers] to be away from people', and he
added that the real problem was not one of site location but of
getting the travellers to conform, finding proper jobs for their
young people, and so on.

Apart from the Conservatives' predictable distaste for the site,
there were objections from Gerald Capper, of the National Gypsy
Education Council, on the grounds that it was remote from the
east end scrap area and from services; from a social worker who
argued that the travellers had expressed a preference for Attercliffe; and from South Yorkshire planning department — on the
grounds that the site would be detrimental to amenity and because
it would create further pressure for development. Since the location is a rural one, it was predictable that the occupational argument should be advanced — namely, that gypsies, as scrap dealers,
should live in an industrial area. There was a strong reaction to the
site proposal from local residents. Several petitions were organized,
and, in April 1976 the Redmire Action Group advertised in a local
newspaper, inviting signatures to a petition from anyone in Shef-

field. In 1978 the group took its case to the high court, bringing an action against the city council to prevent the construction of the site, but the case was dismissed. Following the Conservative victory in the general election in 1979, the local Conservative member of Parliament unsuccessfully tried to persuade the Secretary of State for the Environment to suspend the central government grant for the site, but development continued and it was opened in May 1980.

During 1979 evictions from illegal stopping places were pursued with increasing vigour. In addition to the usual practice of applying for possession orders where eviction attempts were resisted, the city council started to employ security firms to make 'dawn swoops' on the travellers' camps to tow away trailers beyond the city boundary. The boundaries of derelict sites in Darnall and Attercliffe were systematically trenched to prevent occupation and, to further its exclusionary policy, the city council instructed the Department of Health and Social Security office to suspend payments to travellers on illegal stopping places. This aggressive approach to travellers was complemented by a proposal to build a temporary site in the village of High Green, north of the city, on land that had been used formerly as a dump for animal carcasses and is now affected by the seepage of methane. The council's attempts to remove trailers forcibly from the city and deposit them at High Green have been unsuccessful but, as a result of the authority's trenching policy, travellers in Attercliffe are now (March 1980) confined to a single plot of land.

There are several familiar elements in the response to travellers in Sheffield. Prejudiced comment from residents and their elected representatives is generally unrestrained and is reported by the press without qualification, while unsubstantiated allegations of deviancy, often bizarre, contribute to a generally hostile climate. The attitude of councillors, reflecting the views of the electorate, is to press for exclusion with the occasional rider that, when isolated, they can be taught to conform. The response in Sheffield exhibits another characteristic feature, in that travellers have not been consulted about permanent sites. In fact, the chairman of the city's estates committee maintained that 'the gypsies are not entitled to be consulted. It is the council's legal duty to provide a site and we'll provide it where we think best.' The interests of the travellers have hardly registered in the debate, except in negative arguments to the effect that they would be better off elsewhere.

Comparison of the Sheffield case with Hull demonstrates the danger of generalizing from two case studies; the comparison does not increase one's confidence greatly since either may be anomalous. One notable contrast between the two cities is in the location of conflict. The problem in Sheffield has been concentrated in older working-class areas, which throws doubt on my conclusion based on the experience of gypsies in Hull that inner-city areas, unlike peripheral estates, provide a niche for travellers where they will not be subject to working-class antagonism. In fact, several of the evictions in Sheffield were carried out in response to petitions from residents in clearance areas in Attercliffe. This may be explained in part by the fact that the local authority in Sheffield has shown greater hostility towards travellers than the local authority in Hull, as measured by the number of reported evictions in the past five years, which has provided a favourable climate for residents' protests. Sheffield clearly shows greater political autonomy than Hull in ignoring central government advice that travellers should not be harrassed where permanent sites have not been provided. In Sheffield, conflict between travellers and residents has a well defined ideological dimension. Because the problem is localized in a traditional area of Labour support, evictions by a Labour council, coupled with a site proposal for a predominantly Conservative district, work to the advantage of the Labour Party. In the Hull area, most of the middle-class Conservative element of the electorate lives beyond the city boundary, so there is less political advantage to be gained by the Labour Party from harrassing travellers. Here, the dispute is an inter-authority one, and has been projected by some Hull councillors as one between a 'tolerant', Labour-controlled city authority and an 'intolerant' Conservative suburban and rural authority.

These differences in local administration and in the community response may not be particularly important in regard to the travellers' future social and economic status. In both cities, the combination of central government policies designed specifically for travellers, the local response, and changes in urban form suggest increasing confinement and exclusion. There is a similarity in the official policy for site provision in that, in both cities, existing and proposed sites will not meet the needs of all families and in that the locations do not reflect established patterns of movement and settlement. Dissatisfaction is an inevitable outcome of a programme that is dictated by political priorities and ignores the preferences of the travellers.

CHAPTER 11

An alternative view of peripheral status

It is possible to point to several parallels between peripheral groups, in regard to forms of social and economic organization and in their significance as a political issue. High birth rates, low incomes, and identification by the larger society as groups in need of integration, for example, appear to be generally characteristic. In important respects, however, similarities of this sort may be misleading, and the search for parallels can obscure fundamental differences — theoretical inclusion in a group can then do violence to reality. One object of the discussion in the last two chapters was to suggest that to translate the relationship between travelling people and the dominant groups in Western society into a conventional relationship between classes — capital and the supporting state apparatus against labour — denies the possibility that a social group can exist largely apart from the wage labour system *and* from the residual labour force while still not sharing the interests of the bourgeoisie.

In order to get this argument into perspective, it will be useful to compare the relationship between travelling people and mainstream society with the relationship between indigenous minorities and the industrial state, minorities whose economies have been traditionally based on land and marine resources. This comparison should demonstrate that there are variants of outsiderness some of which can be accommodated without difficulty in a Marxist model while others cannot. I will suggest that the peripheral condition of nomadic and semi-nomadic urban minorities and indigenous, land-based minorities differs in one important respect: namely, the degree to which they control their economic relationship with the larger society. In the case of gypsies, their contact with settled society is essential to their economy and represents a logical adjustment to the urbanization process. In relation to the dominant society, they have themselves assumed an active and dominating role, one that is underplayed or ignored in the modernization literature. Groups like the Canadian Eskimo, by contrast, have suffered a progressive disruption of their traditional economy, first with the expansion of the capitalist market system into their homelands and then with the development of extractive industry, which generates a temporary demand for labour but contributes to greater dependence. The Eskimos' dependence on urban, industrial society has increased, but it has not been sought.

It is this characterization of peripheral minorities that has tended to be applied globally, both in bourgeois and Marxist guises and it is inappropriate when applied to gypsies. There is evidence, furthermore, that the dependency thesis is not entirely adequate as an account of the outsider status of indigenous minorities. Groups such as the Canadian Eskimo may control some resources that provide a basis for economic autonomy, although these are often unrecognized or devalued by white society; and they continue to retain a cultural boundary between themselves and the dominant system, which is manifested in their resistance to modernizing forces. In this respect, gypsies and, say, Eskimos have some affinities as peripheral groups. We might consider the dependency and autonomy arguments as pessimistic and optimistic views, respectively, and I will examine them in turn in this chapter.

Before considering the empirical evidence, I would point to what appears to be one global characteristic of the problem: the concern of the state with the regulation of the social and economic life of peripheral ethnic groups, both in the state's own interests and in the interests of industrialists. This obviously contributes to the persistence of outsider status, but the programme of regulation elicits different responses in different groups, according to the material basis of their culture and, more generally, their world-structure. Again, this problem is related to the issue of autonomy, which the comparison of gypsy communities in industrial states and indigenous minorities should clarify.

In an attempt to argue these points, I will concentrate in this chapter on the relationship between native peoples and the dominant society in the Arctic and sub-Arctic areas of North America (Canada and Alaska). The history of contact in this zone is probably similar in important respects to that experienced by the Australian aboriginal population, the native American in the co-terminous United States, and the native peoples of the Soviet north, for example. The attraction of the North American Arctic as a case study is that much of the economic development of the area is recent and well documented, as are the consequent social changes. From a theoretical standpoint, the region is a useful one to consider because there is a clear connection between major industrial development and forms of social organization that embrace the native population — in fact, adjustment to economic development is a major element of social policy. This is essentially an ideological problem, manifested, for example, in the settlements designed for native communities. The creation of planned environments for native peoples and for British gypsies are parallel developments, both of which have been projected as attempts to redistribute resources in favour of poor minorities; and, as with sites for gypsies, the form of the provision for the indigenous population of the Arctic can be criticized for failure to take account of a distinctive culture. The comparison is useful in understanding the form, objectives and social consequences of what are effectively institutional environments.

The account begins with a general description of the population distribution and location of industrial resources in Alaska and the Canadian Arctic, providing a necessary but unexciting prelude to a discussion of the exploitation of the native population by the dominant white society. Whereas the previous analysis of conflict between gypsies and the settled society focused on large urban centres, we are concerned here primarily with small settlements in a very large area, which might be thought to disqualify the problem from inclusion in the urban category. The subject matter is urban, however, in the sense that development policies for the North emanate from the metropolitan areas of the United States and Canada; urban forms and institutions are projected into a rural area, and an urban economy is superimposed on a rural economy. The problem examined in this chapter is essentially one of incursions by southern capital into this rural periphery and the consequences of these developments for the indigenous population. However, I will also touch on the problems affecting native minorities in larger cities in the sub-Arctic, in Alaska and outside the region, in Canada. There is a contrast between planned native settlements in the Arctic and native adaptations to southern cities that is in some respects similar to that between British gypsy sites and urban gypsy communities. An examination of this similarity should provide a further demonstration of the different social, economic and political processes that can contribute to the peripheral position of ethnic minorities.

POPULATION DISTRIBUTION AND TRENDS[1]

The arctic and sub-Arctic regions of North America have a low biological productivity, while extractive industry is capital-intensive and uses little labour after the development phase, with the result that, even with large-scale investments, very large areas are able to support only small human populations. The North-West Territories of Canada, for example, had a total population of about 42,000 in 1976, with a gross density of only 0.01 persons per square mile. Most of this population was concentrated in small settlements — Yellowknife (8,200), Hay River (3,200), Inuvik (3,000), Fort Smith (2,300) and Frobisher Bay (2,300) were the largest. The Yukon had a population of about 21,000 in 1976 and the largest urban centre in the Canadian North — Whitehorse, had a population of about 13,000. The native population of the North-

---

1 The statistical information comes from the censuses of Canada and the United States and is tabulated in Armstrong, Rogers and Rowley (1978).

West Territories and the Yukon was approximately 40 per cent of the total, comprising 14,000 Inuit (Eskimos) and possibly 15,000 from other ethnic groups, primarily Indians (Dene) and Metis (mixed-race, with Indian blood). An additional 5,000 Inuit lived in Quebec and Labrador. The largest white populations were in the biggest towns, where natives are a minority, but natives were numerically dominant in smaller settlements. In spite of being the largest group in some settlements, however, the native population has become increasingly dominated in a political and economic sense by whites; urbanization has been a crucial element in the incorporation of the Inuit and Indian populations into the industrial economy.

In Alaska the situation is somewhat different, in that the largest urban centres are much larger than in the Canadian Arctic. In 1976 the population of Anchorage was about 185,000 and of Fairbanks, including Fairbanks North Star Borough, 82,000. These places had considerable primacy in the state's urban system, however, the next largest being Kenai, including Kenai Peninsula Borough, with a population of 22,000, followed by Juneau and Ketchikan, each with populations about 19,000. A spatial concentration of native minorities was noticeable in Fairbanks, although not, apparently, in Anchorage (according to Jones, 1974); and, as in the Canadian North, natives constituted a majority only in small settlements.

The 1970 census indicated that the native population of Alaska — 28,000 Inuit, 16,600 Indians and 6,600 Aleuts — made up only 18 per cent of the state's total, although all these indigenous groups had much higher rates of natural increase than the white population owing to a high birth rate and declining mortality. The most striking characteristic of demographic change in the state is the high rate of urbanization of the native population. Thus, in the period 1939–70, the urban percentage in the south-east region, including Anchorage, increased from 28.7 to 59.0 and in the south-central region, which includes Fairbanks, from 4.3 to 54.5 per cent. Corresponding trends for non-natives were 71.2 to 84.2 per cent in the south-east and 30.5 to 68.1 per cent in the south-central region. These figures might suggest increasing participation of natives in the urban economy, but this would be a premature conclusion. An assessment of the economic and social benefits derived from the urban experience will require an analysis of the roles of native peoples in the workforce and a comparison of the capitalist system with the subsistence and trading economy.

In general, the Arctic and sub-Arctic regions of North America have witnessed in recent years a disruption of small, stable, native communities through the immigration of whites concerned with the exploitation of industrial resources and with the administration of an increasingly complex bureaucracy. Contact between mercantile/industrial societies and the native communities had been made as early as the seventeenth century, when some trade links were established, and this contact occasionally had catastrophic consequences for the indigenous populations, notably through the introduction of diseases to which they had no resistance and the depletion of staple food resources, such as whales. However, the permanent presence of a dominant and alien white population and the large-scale appropriation of resources by companies from the metropolitan south is essentially a feature of the last 20 years.

THE WHITE AND NATIVE ECONOMIES

For southern, urban economies, the Arctic and sub-Arctic have assumed primary importance as resource zones that provide raw materials required for industrial expansion. It is what Rea (1976) has called 'the hard frontier', because of the difficulty involved in extracting resources and because of what might be termed 'the challenge'. The mineralized Shield rocks of the North-West Territories, the Yukon plateau and the northern cordillera contain a range of high-value minerals, including gold, silver, nickel and platinum, and large reserves of copper, lead and zinc. In addition, the sedimentary basins, particularly the North Shelf of Alaska and the Mackenzie Delta, have major reserves of oil and natural gas. The exploitation of these resources, however, is hampered by distance from markets which renders the exploitation of some low value—high bulk minerals, such as iron ore, uneconomic or, at best, marginal. As Brody (1973) has observed, mineral exploitation in the High Arctic is possible only if the reserves are massive and of high quality and market prospects look good in the long term.

Because development costs in the Arctic are very high, it is generally beyond the capacity of individual companies to exploit reserves, so that development typically involves international consortia and national governments. The magnitude of development costs is illustrated by Brody's example of the Cominco Corporation, which spent $2 million in evaluating an ore body on Cornwallis Island; a characteristic example of an industrial organization is the Panarctic combine, a consortium of oil companies in which the Canadian government had a 45 per cent equity interest, formed in 1968 to undertake oil and gas prospecting in the High Arctic. The involvement of the state is important in that it minimizes the risk to individual investors and it signifies official faith in the 'new frontier'. Development clearly occurs on the assumption that there will be continuing expansion of the resource base of industrial society so that massive investments of capital are justified. Some of these enterprises are marginal, however, being vulnerable to downturns in the economy that might be caused, for example, by a steep rise in the price of oil; the substitution of materials; capital-switching, as when the oil companies transferred their attention from the Arctic to the North Sea; and the overoptimistic estimation of reserves.

In other words, despite government subventions, long-term investment in the northern economy is not assured and the best that the state can do is to moderate the variable pattern of production that would have occurred with no government intervention. Armstrong, Rogers and Rowley (1978) give an instance of the kind of short-term mineral exploitation that has particularly adverse consequences for the native population. The mining of high-grade nickel—copper ore was started at Rankin Inlet in the Keewatin district, in the eastern part of the North-West Territories, in 1957, at the rate of 250 tonnes a day. Inuit were given official encouragement to seek employment at the mine and a number of families

Table 2

Work experience of Alaskan males (percentage of workers 39—40 years old in 1970)

	White	*Non-white**
	%	%
Non-worker, 1965	2.1	27.3
Non-worker, 1970		
Non-worker, 1965	7.9	13.8
Worker, 1970		
Worker, 1965	6.4	20.3
Non-worker, 1970		
Worker, 1965	83.6	38.6
Worker, 1970		

*Includes some non-natives
Source: Armstrong *et al.* (1978).

moved to Rankin Inlet from other settlements. When the mine closed, in 1962, the area was not good for hunting, so the local Inuit became dependent on welfare. Thus, the federal government, having encouraged the investment, was subsequently required to mitigate the effects of closure on the native workforce.

The evidence collected by Brody (1975), Usher (1976b) and others suggests that this is not an isolated instance, and that the effect of major investments on the native population is in many respects detrimental even for families who gain materially from wage labour. First, it is evident that the Inuit and Indians are marginal participants in the labour force. If, for example, we compare the work experience of a group of Alaskan native and white males for the period 1965—70 (table 2), it is evident that unemployment and short-term employment were much more serious problems for natives than whites, although the official definition of employment probably gives a misleading impression of the economic activity of the native population in that some forms of work that they engage in are not included in the official categories. These statistics, however, are consistent with the view that the involvement of the native population in the capitalist mode of production has resulted in their assuming a lumpenproletarian status. Mooney's (1976) analysis of the Coastal Salish in British Columbia points to the same conclusion: in comparison with the white working class living in similar residential areas in Vancouver, the Indian population had an inferior economic status and was over-represented in the residual workforce. Hugh Brody is quite emphatic about the impact of the capitalist system on the social structure and economy of the Inuit in the High Arctic:

If separated from his own means of production and unable to have a sure relationship to the intruder's means of production, the Eskimo — like many American and Canadian Indians before him — will be turned into a migrant worker, a casual labourer and — as the lumpenproletarian condition develops — prostitute, thief and beggar. [Brody, 1975]

Specifically, there are a number of damaging consequences of involvement with large-scale extractive industry. The effects of such large-scale investments are generally disruptive and may lead in the long run to a dependence on urban, industrial society. First, investment by an oil or mining company creates opportunities for manual work. Natives who gain employment on big projects can obtain wages that are much higher than the *money* incomes that are otherwise available in the local economy, but the work may require migration and long periods away from home. On the Arctic island oil and gas sites, for example, workers can be away for 20 days in each month (Brody, 1977).[2] Second with the money earned on labouring jobs, Inuit are able to buy hunting equipment, such as high-powered rifles with telescopic sights, out-

---

2 For a mainstream White view of the socio-psychological aspects of industrial development, see Stevenson (1968). In discussing the migration of the Inuit to industrial jobs in southern communities, Stevenson emphasizes problems of maladjustment and comprehension. The latter is concerned with a knowledge of 'acceptable social behaviour' in regard to drinking, sanitation, responsibilities to an employer and so on.

board motors and expensive skidoos (motor-powered sledges), which makes them more efficient hunters than those who hunt by traditional methods. Berger (1977) concludes that cash income from labouring jobs has reinforced native culture where the money has been used to buy hunting equipment, but several writers who have observed recent changes in the native economy emphasize the divisive effect of cash income on the community and a move to dependence on the externally controlled cash economy. As Novak (1975) found, in his study of the Nunivagamiut in Alaska, hunters have become highly dependent on the products of Western technology and, consequently, dependent on cash income to purchase and maintain their equipment. Significantly, poor families were unable to participate in hunting activities because of prohibitive capital costs, and thus had to rely on store-bought food. Brody and Novak suggest that hunting as a way of life loses its appeal since traditional methods demonstrably produce less food from the land than hunting with modern equipment. At the same time, the wage labourer is less inclined to hunt since his wages are adequate to buy processed food from the store, so that families in general become more dependent on the money economy.

The development of an externally controlled servicing sector is an important factor contributing to economic dependency. Retail prices, particularly for food, are high, and a poor family in the Canadian North or Alaska that was mainly dependent on the supermarket would need to spend a large proportion of its income on food. In 1978 a Canadian Broadcasting Corporation consumer programme reported that a basket of groceries costing $40 in Montreal and Ottawa, $42 in Toronto and $46 in Vancouver would cost $54 in Yellowknife, $58 in Inuvik and $67 in Frobisher Bay (*The Drum,* Inuvik, 1 March 1978). Similarly, at Mekoryuk, on Nunivak Island, store prices for food were two to three times as high as in Seattle (Novak, 1975). Within the Arctic, considerable price variations exist between larger and smaller settlements. Usher (1976a) noted higher prices for red meat in the small and predominantly native settlements of Aklavik and Tuktoyaktuk than in the administrative centre of Inuvik, owing to the addition of freight charges.

Obviously, high prices for food must be set against high wages on industrial projects, but when construction or mining projects terminate and work is no longer available, it is difficult for a native family to return to the traditional hunting and trading economy because radical economic change also alters social relationships. The effect of the intrusion of southern capital is to transform the egalitarian native community, in which wealth in the form of food is shared so that no family will go hungry as long as there is food in the camp, into a stratified society, in which the sharing ethic no longer holds. The argument is that the introduction of capital-intensive industry initiates an irreversible process of cultural change. This is suggested, for example, by D. G. Smith's (1975) analysis of ethnic relations in the Mackenzie delta, in which he identifies a divide within the native community between those who have modernized and those who retain traditional values. Thus, we have the creation of a fragmented working class. Although some Inuit try to go back to the hunting economy, having appreciated the detrimental effects of the southern economic system on their well-being, as Brody (1975) observed in Frobisher Bay, where the Inuit tried to establish a hunting camp outside the settlement despite high earnings from industrial employment, this is very difficult to achieve once the population has been incorporated into the proletariat. Recent comments by Inuit would support this view (reported in *The Drum*, Inuvik, 25 January 1978):

Hugh McCallum and Tony Clark of Project North should come north now and tell the 65 or 70 people of Coppermine who are now unemployed that they should go back to the land and see what kind of reaction they will get. This year, the seal skin prices are down and everywhere in the Arctic, trappers are not getting the catches of white fox that they used to over the past few years. . . . We have little to fall back on now that the oil industry is doing as little as it is.

> [Inuit in a speech to the legislature, NWT, 8 February 1978]

L.P. (High Arctic) told his colleagues that hunting seals was no longer worth it for the Inuit. He commented that returns of two dollars a pelt could not buy ten pounds of sugar or even one can of milk.

> [Report on a meeting of the Council of the NWT, 8 February 1978]

The second comment is particularly interesting in its implication that dependence on the store in turn devalues the traditional trading economy — presumably, only an industrial wage would be adequate to provide a family with groceries.

Thus, the problem of large-scale industrial development in the North would appear to be that (1) industrial employment differentially rewards the native population, creating divisions in the community between 'traditional' and 'modern' and devaluing the traditional economy; (2) the long-run effect of the intrusion of southern industry is to create a general dependence on cash income, in the form of industrial wages or welfare; but (3) industrial investments tend to be short-term, at least in the sense that they create work for only a short time, resulting, as Rea (1976) observed, in growth without development — mining and construction projects do nothing for regional economic autonomy. Thus, when industrial projects are run down, there is nothing left except welfare and high-priced consumer goods.

In the circumstances, it is understandable that residents of the North should call for the investment of local capital in industries that will give stability in the regional economy. As an editorial writer in *The Drum* put it,

With inflation over 10 per cent, unemployment as high as 20 per cent, we in the North would be well advised to consider local manufacturing and resource industries if we wish to maintain our standard of living. Too much dependence on the oil industry has now fractured our economic balloon. [*The Drum*, Inuvik, 25 January 1978]

With small and scattered markets and little indigenous capital, prospects cannot be good — a parka manufacturing plant in Inuvik employing from 40 to 50 people stands out as a newsworthy industrial development. One alternative, advocated by Rea (1976), for example, is to develop employment in the public service sector, particularly in the social services and education. This can be criticized, however, on the grounds that reliance on the public sector only perpetuates external control and ensures the continuing dependence of the native population on white institutions,

while public sector employment is susceptible to changes in policy
in regard to the regional and sectoral allocation of resources. Since
private capital, with the support of government, is primarily
responsible for the dependent status of the indigenous population,
public investment in the service sector may appear as the only
realistic alternative, but it does not give the Inuit or the Indians
control over their own resources. Kunitz (1977), in his study of
the employment structure on the Navajo reservation in New
Mexico and Arizona, identifies the problem in these terms. Control of private business was largely in white hands — three-quarters
of all businesses licenced by the Navajos were run by non-Navajos,
while federal support was concentrated on the provision of social
service jobs, such as teachers' aides and alcoholism aides. Support
for economic development programmes was resisted by local white
politicians on the grounds that such aid was 'socialistic', and
spending on social services was politically less sensitive. The reservation was effectively a colony, and the emphasis on job creation
in the social services, which provided two-thirds of all employment
in 1974, served to reinforce colonial status.

On the evidence reviewed here, we might agree with Brody
(1977) that the intrusion of southern capital and state involvement in the sub-Arctic and Arctic, what he terms 'the total intrusion effect', has caused an irreversible breakdown in the subsistence
and trading economy. This view is consistent with Berger's
(1979a) assertion that 'nothing smashes tradition, makes obsolete
and denies the past as continually and thoroughly as the capitalist
mode of production. "It is not communism that is radical, but
capitalism", as Brecht said.' The rate of change unleashed by the
North Atlantic domination of the world, Berger argues, denied
universality, and introduced discontinuity as normal.

THE EVIDENCE FOR AUTONOMY

This analysis may be unduly pessimistic. Several writers who have
made emphatic statements about the dependence and low econ-

omic status of the native population, in particular Brody and Usher, have at the same time recognized elements of economic independence and cultural autonomy that cannot be captured by official statistics on employment and wealth. The weight that should be attached to the native economy in modifying the picture of domination by external interests is clearly problematic, and, as with travelling people, as assessment of economic status is made difficult by the contrast in world-views between the indigenous population of the North and mainstream society in metropolitan Canada and the United States. Usher, for example, suggests that:

The hinterland (that is, that area settled by the Inuit, Dene, and Metis) is more than a special case of the working class or underclass [*sic*] in that it consists of regions and peoples having, to a greater or lesser degree, territorial integrity and distinctive ways of life. Hence, these people have special interests not necessarily shared by the metropolitan working class. [Usher, 1976b]

Notwithstanding the vagueness of this statement and the undefined distinction between 'metropolitan working class' and other working-class groups, Usher evidently recognizes an ethnic or racial dimension to the problem which he has difficulty in reconciling with a Marxist model of class conflict.

The first, and most important, element of the world-structure of the native Northerners that sets them apart from the industrial workforce is their relationship to the traditional mode of production. This can be dismissed, as it is, for example, by Rea (1976), who refers to the 'extremely low and uncertain income levels in ... traditional employments [*sic*]'. Brody (1977) cites Hobart's evidence to the Berger Inquiry, in which he quoted *per capita* incomes for the Inuit, Dene and Metis in the Mackenzie Delta region at near or below $1,000, compared, say, with a white teacher's salary of $12,000–$14,000, which would confirm Rea's view. It may be significant that Hobart was an expert witness called by an oil company which would have an interest in undervaluing the traditional economy since it would then be able to argue that pipeline construction would provide the only alternative source of employment for the native population.

There is, now, a considerable amount of evidence that hunting, fishing and the collection of wild foods such as berries can make a major contribution to the native economy, with variations obviously depending on the resource base, although its significance is rarely appreciated by outsiders. As Berger (1977) comments, 'The fact is, the native economy exists *out of sight* of the white people.' The problem appears to be a general one, namely, that the dominant system can interpret the 'hidden' economic system of minorities only through a rigid categorical framework which is derived from the forms and relationships of the industrial state so that the real significance of activities or resources to the minority group is obscured. Ingold (1976) illustrates the point nicely in his discussion of the employment problems of the Skolt Lapps. He notes that Skolts became unemployed only after a state employment agency was set up in 1964 and, further, that to be classified as unemployed is a desirable condition, since it allows a person to keep up traditional activities while receiving sufficient income from unemployment compensation to buy additional food, materials or hunting equipment. To the dominant society, the only alternative to unemployment is a regular job, but this would disturb the Skolt adaptation to the dominant system since it would not leave enough time for hunting. Thus, Ingold suggests a subsistence subsidy to replace unemployment benefit with no obligation to find work.

In a similar vein, Berger (1977) recounted a major discrepancy in the evidence of native people and a white Canadian research team — Gemini North, under contract to Arctic Gas — in regard to the significance of trapping in the Northern economy. He comments:

To Gemini North, and to most white people, trapping is a job, much the same as any other job. So determining the number of trappers is simply a matter of counting how many people during the period of the survey ran a trap line and sold furs. The native people, however, do not see trapping as a job; it is, rather, a way of life based on the land and its resources. Running a trap line is but one of a number of seasonal activities. [Berger, 1977]

The same opposition of views on the role of work is noted by D. G. Smith (1975) in his study of native—white relationships in the Mackenzie Delta. Again, we have a similarity with British travelling people in that a number of complementary sources of income characterize the minority economy but, commonly, only a single occupation is recognized by members of the dominant society, and the response to the minority stems partly from this conception.

Rather than dismissing traditional ways of making a living as activities that wither away in the course of modernization, hunting and gathering should be recognized as a basic element in the native economy. It is possible to approximate the value of 'country foods' in cash terms by giving them the value of substitutable items in the market economy, such as red meat in the case of wild game. On this basis, Usher (1976a) has estimated that a modest harvest for a family — say, a dozen caribou, 60 geese and 230 kilogrammes of fish in a year — would have a cash value of $6,200, while a wage labourer hunting only at weekends could supplement his family's income by as much as $2,800. From this and similar analyses, Brody (1977) estimates that household incomes at the time of the Berger Inquiry (1972) ranged from $4,350 to $10,000, which suggests that Hobart's estimates of *per capita* incomes, for Dene at $839.64, for Inuit at $666.89 and for Metis at $1,146.52, are considerable underestimates (note the spurious sense of precision indicated by figures to two places of decimals).

Further evidence in support of Brody and Usher comes from Novak's (1975) study of the subsistence economy on Nunivak Island, Alaska. He found that, over a four-month summer period, the Inuit in the settlement of Mekoryuk obtained from slightly less than half to three-quarters of their food from the land and the sea, although it should be pointed out that the island was particularly rich in marine food resources. Further, Novak emphasizes that this level of consumption of country foods was dependent on having enough cash income to buy hunting equipment, so income from wage labour was necessary for successful hunting — elsewhere in this region, Inuit were too poor to hunt successfully. This contradicts Brody's view that the cash economy has a disruptive

and, in the long run, debilitating effect on the traditional economy, but Novak's observations were possibly made over too short
a period for him to reach a reliable conclusion in regard to the full
impact of wage labour on the subsistence economy. He does not,
for example, consider the effect of wage employment on kin
group responsibilities, particularly the sharing of food. None the
less, these studies, and other described in the Berger Report, confirm that traditional hunting activities play an important part in
the native economy. As Usher recognizes, it is not sufficient to
measure the value of country food in cash terms, even where
realistic substitution costs can be estimated, although such exercises do help to modify beliefs about the deprivation of native
peoples.

As important as the contribution of wild food to the domestic
economy is the attachment to the land that hunting and fishing
signify, and this attachment is of vital importance in resisting incorporation by the metropolitan south and in retaining cultural
autonomy. As Berger discovered from the Dene at Fort Franklin,
people still use their ancestral land base for hunting, although
migration between camps has been replaced by hunting trips from
the settlement using snowmobile, boat or chartered plane. Technological adaptations, which indicate superficially a transition to the
mainstream, can contribute to the cultural continuity and stability
of the community. As I have argued above, however, this benefit
from contact with industrial society may be negated by the
economic inequalities and social divisions that result from dif-
ferential rewards to the native population and by the inherently
short-term interest of capital in the native as a worker. For this
reason, it seems contradictory to argue, as Berger does in the
introduction to his report, that 'the legitimate claims and aspira-
tions' of the native peoples can be honoured at the same time as
the industrial system exploits gas, oil and other mineral resources
in the Arctic — these are conflicting goals. The first objective
would be realized only if the advanced industrial economies cur-
bed their expansionist activities and acknowledged the necessity
for a reduction in living standards or, rather, reduction in levels of
material consumption.

SETTLEMENT AND HOUSING

The legitimation of metropolitan domination

The incorporation of the indigenous minorities in the North into industrialized society is expressed in the growth of wage labour and unemployment, but it is also manifested in the development of a settlement pattern that embodies metropolitan standards and conceptions of order and produces the inequalities that characterize the dominant society. As an illustration of the incorporation process, I will consider in this section the official view of the housing and settlement problem, critical comments on official policy, and the native response. Somewhat distinct from this question is the experience of indigenous northerners in big cities, particularly in Alaska and in southern Canada, where there are existing or incipient ghetto communities. There is an obvious difference of size and complexity of place to which the Inuit or Dene have to adjust, in the form of contact that the native has with traditional culture and environment, and in the level of involvement with the social control and welfare agencies. While the economic position of the native in the sparsely populated Arctic and the big cities has the same structural basis, it is only in the small, planned settlements that the objective of control through environmental design can be realized since most of the building stock is provided by the public sector. It is in the small Arctic settlements that we have an interesting analogy to the gypsy site question in Britain.

Settlement and housing programmes

A concentration of population is generally considered desirable by governments for efficient administration and welfare, particularly for regions or for groups of the population that are seen as deprived. Settlement policies in the old coal mining area of north-eastern England, in Durham and Northumberland, for example, were for a long period designed to concentrate population in order to provide better access to shopping, education and welfare services, notwithstanding the preferences of the residents in the mining villages. In general, the benefits of living in larger settlements, which are self-evident to planners, may not be recognized by the client population.

In the North American Arctic and sub-Arctic, trading posts and missions have provided a focal point for migrants since the nineteenth-century, but the movement of population into settlements on a permanent basis has occurred more recently. In the Canadian north, Brody (1975) describes a process of increasingly prolonged stays in settlements with a concomitant breakdown of semi-nomadic camp life. This movement to settlements was apparently precipitated by the establishment of schools, which led to the unacceptable separation of parents from children if the parents stayed in the camps. In addition, some forms of welfare were available from religious orders and the government, and this constituted an attraction. As Brody suggests, there were 'informal and diverse pressures', involving, on the one hand, the advertising of settlements as desirable because of the availability of health services, education and food stores, and, on the other, criticism of camp life by the settlement administrators as unhealthy and as a mode of living that made it impossible for children to receive an education. When the welfare housing programme was begun in the North-West Territories in 1956, residence in settlements became obligatory if Inuit were to be able to take advantage of the programme, thus creating more pressure for population concentration. For the white administration, the settlement had the explicit objective of encouraging acculturation and integration, since the Inuit culture was judged to be inferior.

Thus, A. B. Yates, Director of the Northern Economic Development Branch of the Canadian Department of Indian Affairs, in an account of official policy written in 1970, asserted that:

The housing programme is . . . only one step, albeit an essential one, in the progress of the Eskimo people. By taking it, they will begin to adapt to the more sophisticated communities that will develop as the potential of the non-renewable resources of northern Canada is realized. [Yates, 1970]

Several points emerge from Yates's paper, which might be taken to represent a general bureaucratic, conformist view of minorities.

First, there is a concern with standards. A survey of Inuit housing in the mid-1960s showed general overcrowding — 'minimum *acceptable* standards indicate a limit of two persons in a one room dwelling' (my emphasis). Second, there is a presumption that the goals of the minority community are changing — 'health, education, and housing are now the primary goals' (but who decided on these goals?). Third, rental housing, along with other welfare programmes, will provide *economic* benefits. The life based on renewable resources was considered not to be economically viable, and any future prosperity was dependent on concentration in settlements where the residents would be well placed to benefit from the job opportunities created by non-renewable resource exploitation. Thus, we have the devaluation of tradition and the assertion that acceptance of the fruits of industrialization provides the only way forward. Health problems among the Inuit provided an initial impetus for the housing programme and gave it a legitimate function in the eyes of southern Canadians, but there is evidence that the advance of Western technology and metropolitan values in the North has created as many health problems as it has solved, particularly in its contribution to alcoholism. Even Yates's health statistics, included to demonstrate the value of the rental housing programme in the reduction of respiratory and digestive diseases, are unconvincing.[3] This perspective on the indigenous population is supported, for example, by Honigman (1973), who acknowledges the economic and political domination of whites in northern settlements but argues that this exploitation makes the native people 'physically [*sic*], economically, and socially marginal' and sees a solution to this problem lying in education so that the Inuit, Dene and Metis will be better able to participate in decision-making and to accept administrative responsibility. Ørvik (1976), writing about the Inuit in Greenland, presents an identical perspective on the problem. He argues, as Yates implied, that most natives desire modernization, meaning incorporation in the industrial

---

3 His case is based on statistics for four years, and the only categories of disease included are respiratory and digestive. For digestive diseases, the incidence, measured in patient days, increased for three years and fell only in the fourth.

state, and that there is no alternative model of development. Since there is no alternative, it is necessary to facilitate modernization by providing social services, and the provision of services requires the relocation of population in settlements. He describes the Danish government's policy of concentrating population by building four- or five-storey apartment blocks which comply with Danish standards and allow the efficient administration of medical and social services. While admitting that the native population is not entirely happy in its new environment, discontent is attributed to defects in planning and administration rather than to the questionable suitability of the programme for native welfare. For example, in regard to the exclusion of natives from decision-making, Ørvik suggests that 'The detailed planning and preparation necessary for the advances, require a degree of expertise and special insight which few, if any, native leaders have; and the display of such capacities by white peoples has served to demonstrate to the natives how backward they are.'

CRITICAL VIEWS OF SETTLEMENT POLICIES

The ideological basis of the settlement programmes in northern Canada and in Greenland is obvious — it is assumed in these schemes that domination of minorities by the capitalist state is legitimate and is the only pattern of development that will increase the welfare of the native populations. Yates and Ørvik echo the modernization myth, namely, that there is an inevitable transition from a subsistence and trading economy to an industrialized, technology-intensive one, and that this change is accompanied by changes in status systems, in forms of family and kinship organization and in political behaviour. If these changes occur, then housing designed to standards applicable to the dominant society will be acceptable to the minority group and will be preferred by them to indigenous forms of shelter. An alternative view, represented, for example, by Thomas and Thompson (1972) in their review of the housing programme in the Canadian north, is that such a policy is highly ethnocentric — 'a massive effort to

employment opportunities which disrupt the traditional economy and social relations and confer lumpenproletarian status on the native worker, and, second, by concentrating the population in settlements that are designed to reproduce the class structure of the dominant society and from which control is more easily exercised. The simplicity of the built form of settlements contrasts with the complexity of traditional shelter forms, where there is a conjunction of several activities in the same place and an untidiness that is anathema to southern administrators (Davis, 1977). The contrast is essentially that identified by Turner (1976), namely, that 'the bureaucratic system produces things of a high standard [possibly] at a great cost, and of dubious value, while the autonomous system produces things of extremely varied standard, but at low cost, and of high use-value'.

NATIVE PEOPLES IN THE CITY

The previous account has been concerned with changes that have occurred within the regions of physical resource exploitation, where the Inuit and other groups have experienced the impact of the industrial state on their traditional cultures. There has been migration to small urban centres dominated by whites, for example to Inuvik, but this population relocation has taken place at the intra-regional level. Thus, the native peoples have not been cut off from their resource base by physical distance and, in many cases, have been able to combine hunting with occasional wage labour – to an extent, they have been able to resist incorporation into the dominant system.

Incorporation has another dimension, however, in the movement of native peoples, particularly Dene and Metis, to larger cities, where, for the duration of their stay, they become entirely dependent on income derived from the dominant system, in the form of either wages or, more commonly, welfare. Relocation does not mean a complete break with the rural community, however, since returns to the reservation or settlement are frequent. The city may be seen as an extension of the reserve rather than a place that carries with it associations of modernization and acculturation (Neils, 1971). In other words, native American culture in the city, although supported by a different resource base to that sustaining the indigenous rural population, does not reflect a change in values.

There is a large literature on Indian migrations to cities in the conterminous United States, much of which is concerned with problems of adjustment during a postulated period of modernization. Canada and Alaska have received much less attention in this respect, but there are indications of a minority problem in large urban centres in the sub-Arctic and farther south in Canada, which is developing along predictable lines.

Milan and Pawson (1975), for example, have examined the demographic characteristics of the native population of Fairbanks, Alaska, which is the most northerly large urban centre in North America (1976 population 82,000), with an economic base primarily in public sector activities, notably, the military and government. It is also surrounded by Inuit and Athapaskan villages which are the source of permanent and temporary migrants to the city. The Bureau of Indian Affairs recorded 970 native residents in 1970, but if short-term migrants are added the number increases to about 2,500. If we make an eyeball comparison of Milan and Pawson's map of the spatial distribution of a sample of the native population in Fairbanks with the distribution of properties condemned between 1966 and 1972 (figure 10) (Pearson and Smith, 1975), there is clearly a close association. The clustering of both distributions on the fringe of the central business district suggests an inner-city ghetto where property is being run down or has not been repaired since a flood in 1967. It would appear that we have the combination of a low-income racial minority, which is severely constrained in its choice of accommodation, and a housing market which discourages investments in tenanted properties in the central city.[4] However, according to Jones (1974), there is no similar native enclave in Anchorage, the population being dispersed throughout the borough — a surprising observation.

4 The institutional and market mechanisms that underlie this pattern are discussed in Harvey and Chatterjee (1974).

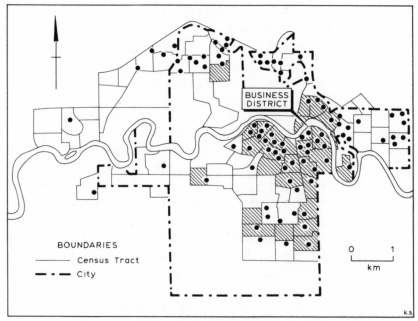

Figure 10   The location of native households in Fairbanks, Alaska, 1970, in relation to sub-standard housing.
(*Sources:* Milan and Pawson, 1975; Pearson and Smith, 1975)

The native population of Fairbanks has the usual characteristics of recent migrants, who have moved for economic reasons. The median age in 1972 was 20.3 for females and 18.4 for males and there were few individuals older than 50. The age-selective nature of migration obviously results in a weakening of kin group relationships which might have provided economic support. Thus, different forms of support are required in the urban environment. That an urban ethnic community can provide substitutes for the mutual supports of the rural community is suggested by studies of skid row communities in Canadian cities. These may paint an extreme picture, which is not necessarily to be accepted as a realistic portrayal of urban native populations in general, but they provide an indication of survival mechanisms that racial minorities can employ if they want to resist incorporation in the 'reserve army'. In any case, we could argue that two characteristics of skid row communities — alcoholism and long-term unemployment, which create a need for mutual aid — are general problems for native peoples in the North, and the spatial concentration of social malaises on skid rows is only a magnification of problems that prevail more widely.

I will comment here on two papers on skid rows, with contrasting methodologies. One, by Rowley (1978), uses a formal survey and questionnaire approach, and the other, by Brody (1971), derives its information from participant observation. Together, they provide a convincing profile of the native skid row resident and establish the function of skid row for the native population. Rowley, working in Winnepeg's skid row, had difficulty in carrying out his survey, particularly, as he put it, 'relating to sampling frames, personal problems, and the basic difficulty in eliciting responses to questionnaire and gaming strategies'. None the less, in two surveys, conducted in the summers of 1974 and 1976, he managed to obtain 150 responses. Of the sample populations, 58 per cent and 57 per cent were Dene or Metis, in 1974 and 1976, respectively, and there was a small number of Inuit in both samples. Caucasians comprised 33 per cent and 37 per cent of the samples. Predictably, there was a high level of long-term unemployment among those under 65 — 86.1 per cent in 1974 and 88.7 per cent in 1976 — but a chi-square test, comparing the unemployment rates for Caucasians and Dene/Metis, showed a significantly higher rate for the latter. In fact, 85 out of 87 Dene and Metis had been without any work in the previous 12 months in 1974 and 80 out of 86 in 1976. This provides some support for Mooney's (1976) contention that, while 'poor whites may occupy an exploited satellite position with respect to greater metropolis powers, the Indians form a satellite within a satellite, exploited to a greater extent'. Further, in noting the persistence of high rates of alcoholism among the native Americans, as high as that of the Caucasians who they are replacing on Canadian skid rows, Rowley speculates that the younger Dene or Metis is disillusioned or despairing, being ill-equipped for economic survival on the reserve, and having his visions of the good life in the city, which stem partly from ideas received at school, shattered by the actual experience of urban unemployment. He is trapped in this environment of bars, pool halls, brothels and hostels.

After his experience as a participant in the skid row community in an unnamed Canadian city, Brody reached similar, but rather more positive, conclusions. Again, the Dene were the dominant group. For them, skid row stood between 'the limitations and constraints of the rural reserve and the rejection and alienation of a white-dominated city life'. Beyond this, however, Brody was struck by the support that skid row offered to the Indian migrant. There was a solidarity among the drinkers in the bars and an established network of bars in the neighbourhood, which contrasted with 'the individuating and isolating qualities of bars outside skid row'. Thus, skid row had well defined boundaries, and sheltered the occupant from the pressures of middle-class, mainstream Canadian life. The distinction of the area from the rest of the city was further emphasized by illegal sources of income and 'indifference to the strictures of puritanism in the larger society'. This served to confirm the prejudices of many whites, who gave the problem a racial complexion. They saw the Indians on skid row as mixed-bloods, which many of them are, and associated virtue only with full-blooded Indians. Thus, the familiar myth of racial purity reinforces the pariah status of the skid row Indian and gives stronger definitions to the neighbourhood boundary. Although the skid row population is alienated from the rest of society, individuals within it are not alienated from each other, since the need to survive creates a high level of interdependence, for example in procuring money for drink and in finding somewhere to sleep for the night. Brody concludes that the skid row Indian is in a lumpenproletarian position to the class system, having no regularized relation to the means of production, dislocated from economic opportunities in the city.

These studies are clearly at variance with those rooted in modernization theory, where skid rows would be interpreted as manifestations of social deviance or adjustment problems. With its clearly demarcated spatial and social boundaries, the Indian skid row community reproduces the reserve, and, given the high rate of seasonal migrations between the city and the reserve (Rowley, 1978) may be considered an outpost of the reserve rather than a distinctly urban phenomenon. As Foraie and Dear (1978) put it, a number of Indians 'have chosen desertion (that is, leaving the reservation for the city in the hope of greater economic opportunity) but [have] since chosen resignation . . . within the urban slum rather than the reserve'.

THE URBAN PROBLEM IN A REGIONAL CONTEXT

In order to get a better perspective on the urban experience, we need to consider further some of the regional problems that affect the Inuit, the Dene and the Metis. First, we should note the emphasis on dependence characterizing much of the literature, which provdes the background for the programmes for regional autonomy advocated by both white and native organizations, such as the Native Brotherhood of Canada in the North-West Territories. Having touched on this problem in discussing the northern economy, it might be useful to enlarge upon the point here and, particularly, to consider the political dimension of the autonomy versus dependency argument. The question might be put like this: can the indigenous population of the North gain control of economic resources and institutions and retain control in the long term? The nature of the resource base that could provide the basis for autonomy will depend on alternative forms that the native economy might take, and this, in turn, will be affected by the political power of the Inuit and Dene to counteract the pressures from southern industrial interests for incorporation. The Alaska Native Claims Settlement Act of 1971 is taken by some as a model for northern development, and it did, at least, signify recognition by the United States government that the native population had legitimate claims to resources which could take precedence over the claims of industrial developers. Under this Act, the native people of Alaska received title to 176,000 square kilometres of land and mineral reserves, plus a cash grant from the federal government and an income, comprising 2 per cent of the annual revenues from mineral leasing activity on state and federal lands. Participation in economic decision-making was furthered by establishing village and regional corporations whose function was to promote development, but all this was in return for relinquishing all aboriginal land claims.

Armstrong, Rogers and Rowley (1978) were favourably impressed by this legislation. They suggest that:

The 1971 Act not only recognized the hereditary claims of Alaska's indigenous minorities and attempted to make restitution for their infringements, but also decreed that these people shall be *equal partners in this larger human experiment*. Not content with high-sounding words alone, it also provided land, money, and corporate organization through which the search for true equality might effectively be conducted. [My emphasis]

What this overlooks is that the development envisaged in the 'larger human experiment' will be concerned primarily with non-renewable resource exploitation, for which the financing and marketing is controlled by a small number of companies and state and private consortia, most of which operate on a world-wide basis. Thus, while the natives will get revenue from mineral exploitation, their organizations will be unable to prevent capital-switching, by which the large corporations achieve profit maximization.

We might contrast this optimistic response to the Act with that of Brody (1977), who considers that 'in political terms . . . a quick settlement was likely to be cheapest'. He suggests that the oil companies and the federal government bought off the Alaskan natives, following pressure from the former, who were anxious to develop the North Slope oil and gas reserves. Berger (1977) concluded that the Inuit and Dene in Canada rejected the Alaskan model because it did nothing to decrease dependence on the non-renewable resource sector. Even in Berger's recommendations, however, the notion of an economic development imperative is retained — he 'proceeded on the asumption that, in due course, the industrial system will require the gas and oil of the western Arctic'. While this is a reasonable assumption, Berger sees it not as contradicting the goal of native self-determination but as a compatible objective.

Finally, Usher (1976b) recognizes the need to give the in-digenous population more power. He suggests that the natives need control over substantial amounts of land, that there should be a slowing down in the rate of petroleum and gas development, that immigration from the south should be controlled, and that locally controlled small-scale industries based on renewable re-sources, and hunting and trapping, should be fostered. A more fundamental proposition is that there should be a re-ordering of southern Canadian society, presumably in the direction of a no-growth economy, in order to reduce the demand for energy, a suggestion that Usher recognizes as unrealistic. Even assuming that a regional development programme that offers more than short-term palliatives can be devised, there would be serious difficulties in putting it into effect because of the unequal power relations in the North. Foraie and Dear apply Bachrach and Baratz's (1970) arguments to the problem of the political impotence of the native population of Canada, noting the dangers of co-optation, outcome modification, intimidation and coercion in political transactions between the minority and the dominant society. In essence, the argument is that, if the minority relies on negotiation to further its ends, the dominant group will not allow a radical alteration in power relations but will devise strategies to manage discontent. The clear implication of these arguments is that domination of the periphery, and of peripheral groups, is an inevitable characteristic of the capitalist state.

CONCLUSION

The research findings reviewed in this chapter are to some extent conflicting, but there does appear to be unanimity in the views of those who have worked closely with native peoples over extended periods. It is evident that the condition of being peripheral to the dominant society does not have a single structural basis, and that settled, indigenous minorities differ from semi-nomadic urban cultures, like gypsies, in regard to the material supports for life and the claims that other groups have on those resources. Thus, although the resource base of the native population in the North American Arctic and sub-Arctic varies considerably, from the rich supplies of wild food around Fort Franklin and on Nunivak Island to the minimal cash supports of skid row residents, all the indigenous peoples have suffered from the spatial expansion of the industrial state into their territory — it is a clear case of internal colonialism. This contrasts fundamentally with travelling people living on the fringe of mainstream society, whose wealth is gleaned from the dominant society and whose resources change as forms of production within the capitalist system change. Their resources are a by-product of capitalist expansion, and, for travellers, being peripheral is necessary rather than being a condition that results from exploitation.

Beyond this, however, there are two similarities between these peripheral groups. The first is the ethnic dimension with which we can associate a distinctive and partly concealed value system, making the outsider group inaccessible to the administrator, employer or academic. Brody refers to the silence and acquiescence of the Inuit in the face of incursions by industrialists into their land, which could be interpreted as acceptance or, at least, lack of hostility to economic development. In fact, the Inuit reject the white man's values while traditionally avoiding conflict. Among travellers, the same attitude to outsiders is expressed in the tendency to agree with propositions put to them by officials and by certain facial gestures in conversation, such as lowering the eyes. The fact that feelings are not articulated, and that economic and social values are partly hidden from the dominant society, provides some protection for the minority group since it helps it to resist manipulation and control. Further, a consciousness of ethnic boundaries, reinforced by economic and political discrimination, sanctions the exploitation of the dominant society, where this is feasible. The negative consequence of muteness, however, is that it contributes to the formulation of inappropriate policies, such as the Inuit educational programme and settlement planning. Approaching the problem from the opposite direction, we could say that the greater understanding of ethnic minorities, which is the object of research, can reveal too much of the world-structure, making the minority more susceptible to manipulation and control.

The second similarity between peripheral groups having different economic relationships to the dominant society is in the official response. It is evident that centralized, hierarchical administrative systems within capitalist social formations, and probably in other social formations, have similar strategies for dealing with non-conformists. Thus, the margin occupied by British travellers is progressively narrowed as land is incorporated into those categories that are considered economically and socially acceptable, making it more difficult for the minority to retain its autonomy. Similarly, the movement of Inuit into settlements, which was not a free and voluntary movement, weakens their relationship with the traditional resource base and creates greater dependency. Mainstream values are imposed on peripheral groups, for example through the medium of trailer sites and houses designed to model standards, which further frustrates their attempts to hold on to the traditional mode of production. The discriminatory nature of these policies is masked, however, by the emphasis on the higher standards that will enable the minority to enjoy the life-style of the majority, and it is easy to appeal to a sense of social justice in providing a deprived ethnic group with bathrooms or electric lighting. This diverts attention from the fact that their resource base and their labour have been appropriated — as Habermas (1976) has argued, 'all class societies must resolve the problem of distributing the social product inequitably and yet legitimately'.

In this analysis, we can identify contradictory forces affecting the economy and social welfare of both travelling people and indigenous groups in the North American Arctic. It might be concluded that, because gypsies have over a long period functioned within the urban economy, and have developed profitable modes of adaptation to the larger system, their position is more secure than that of the Inuit or Dene, who have necessarily occupied a largely passive and dependent role in the capitalist system and have suffered radical disruption of their traditional economy. This optimism about gypsy communities is probably appropriate for countries like the United States, where there is little or no political pressure for regulation, but in Britain and Holland, for example, the capacity of the state to impose severe constraints on the economy and social life of travellers is clear. Thus, it is conceivable that they also will become highly dependent on the dominant society in the long run. This is a difficult case to argue, however, in view of the capacity of travelling people to frustrate the efforts of the state to incorporate them, and it would be wise to suspend judgement.

CHAPTER 12

The outside and the inside

Gypsies, the indigenous populations of North America and similar racial minorities might be considered exceptional in several important respects. The organization of their traditional economies, their social structure and their belief systems set them apart from the rest of the population in advanced industrial societies; this exceptional position is then confirmed and reinforced by the stereotypes of the larger society and by social policy that is informed by these stereotypes. An account of their peripheral status that was concerned only with the labelling process would be insufficient, however, because there are more fundamental factors connected with highly industrialized societies that explain the exclusion of ethnic minorities. I have suggested that the Inuit, for example, are peripheral largely as a result of the demands of the capitalist system, with its need for industrial raw materials, a reserve army of wage labourers and so on. If this is the case, we might ask if other social cleavages within the so-called larger society have a similar structural basis and are manifested in similar forms, particularly in regard to the association of excluded groups with the urban environment.

Although not obviously peripheral in a social or spatial sense, there are groups who would be considered members of the dominant system in relation to indigenous minorities or gypsies that are, in turn, dominated because their needs are imperfectly articulated in the idiom of the dominant group. As Shirley Ardener (1975) suggests, whether a group is dominant or muted depends on the context. Thus, gypsy men may be muted as members of the traveller community, but dominant in their family role. Similarly, the degree of mutedness will vary according to the context. We could suggest that there will be greater communication between groups differentiated by sex or by stage in the life-cycle than there will be between different cultures. To pursue the example of gypsy men and women, in terms of the model of mutedness discussed in chapter 2 we could postulate that there would be a greater degree of overlap in their world-structures, as dominant and muted groups, respectively, than there would be between gypsy women and non-gypsy women. Women in general are not excluded in the sense that gypsies are excluded because they have the capacity to communicate with the dominant male group and the possibility of gaining political power in order to effect changes in the social structure. In other words, we might expect the dominant/muted model to have less general application to groups like women in the larger society with a weaker boundary between the dominant and the excluded group than the boundary that puts distinctively different ethnic minorities on the outside. Ethnic difference, particularly when combined with a different mode of production, strengthens the boundary and minimizes the area of common ground. Where there is a political consciousness of double discrimination, however, membership of two excluded groups may lead to conflicting goals. Gonzales has examined this problem as it affects Mexican American women in the United States. As she recognizes, there is a conflict between the political struggle of the ethnic minority and the political struggle of women, most of whom are members of the group that has oppressed the minority:[1]

Chicanas [Mexican-American women] do not want to sacrifice themselves as the instrument of compromise between Chicanos and the dominant society [but] they must . . . ask themselves if they can become free from the Chicano's

---

1 Gonzales also remarks that research by white academics on Mexican Americans has damaged the interests of Chicanas because it has tended to confirm stereotypical views of the role of women in Chicano society. The problem of ethnocentricity in research by white anthropologists would appear to be a fairly general one.

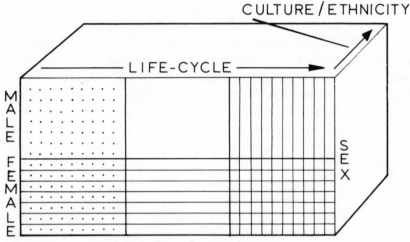

Figure 11   A categorical scheme for muted groups.

anger and frustration through the Anglo-feminist movement, a segment of
the very society which has been the origin of so much of their oppression.
[Gonzales, 1978]

Thus, the ethnic variable complicates the picture of mutedness and
exclusion which we can represent schematically, although somewhat crudely, as in figure 11. In order to demonstrate the parallels
between a mainstream group and a peripheral ethnic minority in
regard to social status and political significance, and thence in relation to their use of the city, I will concentrate in this chapter on
the association between children and urban environments. We can
preface this discussion, however, by considering briefly more
general connections between sex, the life-cycle and mutedness.

   In capitalist social formations, the roles of men and women and
of different age groups are to a considerable degree structured by
the production requirements of such a society, and the partition-
ing of space in the city can be related to these structured roles
because production and the reproduction of the labour force have
specific locational characteristics and generate predictable spatial
relationships. It has been argued, for example, that women in a
capitalist society are assigned a role by the dominant male group,

namely the reproduction of the labour force through child-rearing and servicing the nuclear family. Housewife and mother obviously are not roles occupied exclusively by all women; since some are engaged directly in production, they may have a dual role as producers and as reproducers of the labour force, or they may be single and/or childless. Further, men as fathers are also involved in the reproduction of labour. Although the existence of alternative roles for women weakens the argument that their assigned role is one of social reproduction, it does not invalidate it and discrimination against women may be influenced by the view that a woman's place is in the home. As Foord (1980) observes, the economic recession in Britain has been accompanied by calls for women to give up work and 'withdraw into the family', and it is significant in this respect that female unemployment rates are disproportionately high.

The position of women as a dominated group in capitalist society has clear spatial implications. In the urban case, two obvious problems are the isolation and confinement in residential areas resulting from women's child-rearing and housekeeping functions and the determination of broad land use patterns and communications networks, in the interest of the predominantly male commercial and industrial interests and the male section of the labour force, which creates accessibility problems for women and makes it difficult to combine productive and reproductive activities. The confinement of middle-class women to suburban environments may lead to a particular concern for the purified community — a consciousness of the threatening or polluting nature of social change which may be conveyed to their children, creating a fear of diversity, but this is probably too simple a view. For one thing, the suburbanization of industry brings home and work closer together and makes the combination of production and the reproduction of the labour force easier. Thus, the decentralization of economic activity could be liberating. The corollary of this, however, is that the inner city is losing jobs, so that it becomes increasingly difficult for women on low incomes to combine productive and family roles and the journey-to-work becomes arduous. Black women in North American cities, enduring long journeys to poorly paid domestic employment in white suburbs, represent an extreme example of this problem. The problem of discrimination against women thus has an important class dimension, but there is no doubt that the mutedness of women in general contributes to economic and physical constraint and restricts opportunities in the use of the city because the spatial separation of activities does not coincide with their interests.

A similar argument can be advanced about age or stage in the life-cycle as a determinant of membership of a muted group. Old people and children, in particular, are distinctive because they are not generally valued as labour and, being cut off from the production process, are subject to social and spatial exclusion in several ways. The old obviously have needs that are, in some respects, biologically determined, such as a proximity to services in order to ease the problem of decreased mobility; but, more importantly, they are subject to an arbitrary exclusion from the rest of society through a mandatory retirement age, and this economic exclusion may be reinforced by physical exclusion, indicating a strong classification of stages in the life-cycle (and contrasting markedly with a social structure such as that of travelling people). The problem has an extreme manifestation in the retirement communities in the Sunbelt of the United States, but exists more generally in old people's homes or purpose-built accommodation in local authority housing schemes. The recognition of a hiatus in our knowledge of social space, suggested by studies such as Rowles's (1979) work on old people in the United States, is, in effect, a realization that the old are muted in relation to the dominant group and that this inability to articulate needs in the appropriate idiom is exacerbated by physical and social exclusion. As a social issue, this problem is essentially characteristic of advanced industrial societies, as a cross-cultural view indicates. Munday (1979) notes that in many African societies, although the middle-aged have power, the old have an increasingly important role in the judicial sphere. 'Members of the grandparental generation . . . are growing more and more dependent economically upon their middle-aged sons. The sons, however, are dependent upon their ageing fathers for leadership in the ritual sphere.' I have noted a similar attitude to the old in the gypsy community. The attitude is not one of deference, but old people are treated as equals in the family and basic to this is the continuity of economic life. Neither children nor the old are arbitrarily excluded from work activities, and both older children and grandparents have an important function in caring for young children and babies, freeing others for jobs that require separation from the family, particularly wage labour.

CHILDREN AS A MUTED GROUP

In proposing muteness as a characteristic of certain social groups and of children in particular, Hardman (1973) maintains that there is a basic order of beliefs, values and ideas that bounds one group off from another group. While accepting that sets, or world-structures, defined in these terms have fuzzy boundaries with children, for example imitating adult behaviour in some ways and inevitably moving out of the child category at some point, she argues that 'at the level of behaviour, values, symbols, games, beliefs and oral traditions, there may be a dimension exclusive to the child'. That the child's world is elusive and to some extent hidden from adults is well-established − the Opies' revalations about playground games, for example (Opie and Opie, 1969), indicate marked differences in child and adult world-views. Misinterpretation of this hidden world by adults is inevitably, however. As we grow from child to adult, our conception of the social and physical world changes and our earlier conceptions are forgotten − in a sense, childhood is irretrievably lost once we have left it behind. The reconstruction of childhood by adults is difficult, since the researcher cannot free herself or himself from adult categories in the interpretation of information. As Munday aptly puts it,

The dichotomy adult/child is derived from the adult system of classification and it is only because the distinction exists within the terminology adopted by adults that the category 'child' can be set apart as a subject worthy of study; insofar as children recognize the division and incorporate it into their own models, it is because they have received it from adults. [Munday, 1979]

While we may accept that we cannot really get into the child's world because of the distorting effect of our categorical system, it is, at the same time, safe to assume that children will have distinctive problems and opportunities in coping with the built environment as a result of the difference between adult and child world-structures, however imperfectly the latter may be understood, and that the points of conflict may be recognized.

In considering the relationship between children and the environment in the specific case of the city, it is possible to define distinctive forms of adaptation to the urban environment and constraints that it imposes on children's activities. It is in the form of these adaptations that we can recognize parallels with the peripheral groups discussed formerly and with other minorities.

A recurrent theme of Colin Ward's (1978) book, *The Child in the City,* is that the environments that offer the greatest creative possibilities for children are marginal ones in the sense that they have not completed a transition from one use to another. They are largely unregulated zones where structures and materials can be manipulated or adapted by children. The environments that typically fall into this category are the developing urban fringe and the decaying inner city, although pockets of land of this type may be distributed widely through urban areas. Building materials on partly developed suburban residential sites present obvious opportunities for play, and partly demolished buildings in clearance areas have similar possibilities. Ward describes a run-down area of Cardiff which was for children 'a place of eerie encounters, forbidden games, and for the acting out of destructive passions'. To give an example of the kind of improvization that such an area lends itself to, the growth of cycle speedway in Britain in the 1950s was facilitated by a supply of idle land on the urban fringe, typically land designated for industrial development, where bricks and rubble could be used to mark out a track and adolescents could create some of the excitement of professional speedway for a small outlay on an old pedal cycle.

The importance of such residual spaces is that they are unfinished environments or places in a state of becoming, as Ward puts it. In Bernstein's terms, they are weakly classified so that authority is not particularly concerned with exclusion or boundary maintenance. Thus, they present a haven and a degree of autonomy that the city does not otherwise offer.[2] By contrast, places that are allocated and equipped for play are, in the British case at least, typically ordered, unambiguous and complete – a swing is a swing and has few adaptative possibilities. Adventure playgrounds signify an attempt to weaken the classification of play areas and to cater for the creative and destructive needs of children, but these, again, have limitations stemming from the fact that they are adult interpretations of children's needs.

One characteristic of the marginal space used by children for play, such as areas as derelict housing, is that it is often dangerous; institutional provision of recreational space, by contrast, is ostensibly concerned with safety, although the conventional playground is probably no less dangerous than a building site. This exemplifies the problem wherein a legitimate concern for safety and well-being in practice frustrates the activities of the dependent group. It is analagous to the official concern for standards on permanent sites for travellers, which imposes constraints on the economic and social activities of the residents. In both cases, the user is excluded from design and development.

The residual areas of the city that children can adapt to their own needs are localized and may be inaccessible. Children generally have to cope with an environment that has not been designed for their benefit, and the forms of adaptation that they make may be seen from a dominant perspective as deviant behaviour. We can recognize a number of ways in which children accommodate to unsympathetic aspects of the urban environment and provoke a negative reaction from adults. One aspect of this is the way in which variations in surfaces and changes in level are picked out by children to make their games more interesting. Skate-boarding, for example, was an ephemeral activity that defined its own space, bringing children into conflict with adults where useful slopes also served as footpaths, resulting in an inevitably prohibition of skateboarding in some places and an attempt to contain the sport by

2 In this respect, there is a similarity with squatter settlements in Third World cities, discussed in chapter 9.

building skate-boarding parks. In this, we can see an abhorrence of the mixing of uses and a characteristic response involving the strong classification of the activity in order to reduce conflict. The same need of children to get something out of a hostile environment has more serious manifestations. Ward, for example, notes reports of children burning away the plastic buttons in lifts with gas lighters and opening up the joints on water pipes on local authority estates. Their world-structure is revealed through deviant acts.

It is interesting to compare the relationship between children and adults in industrialized nations, where considerable conflict is evident, with the relationship obtaining in Third World countries. Ward (1978) asserts that 'juvenile vandalism is a phenomenon of the rich countries of the world'. It is significant that, among the poor majority in Third World societies, childhood is not bounded and separated from adulthood as it is in industrialized nations. In particular, productive work is a necessary and legitimate activity for children and serves to integrate them into the adult world. Clearly, much of the work undertaken by children in poor countries is necessary only because of the extreme inequality in incomes between the (few) rich and the rest of the population, which makes it difficult for poor families to survive without a productive contribution from children.

This does not mean, however, that productive work, as distinct from formal education, is necessarily bad. As I suggested in discussing the gypsy economy, work has educational value in the context of gypsy culture, and to devalue children's contribution to scrap sorting or vehicle maintenance by giving priority to mainstream, formal education is an ethnocentric judgement. Munday (1979) draws the same conclusion from a comparison of children in Britain and in African societies. She maintains that British children are sheltered from the outside world and are rarely entrusted with any responsibility. In particular, a child's engaging in the adult world of work to any significant extent is regarded as exploitation. Economic independence, she argues, undermines the power relationship within the family, and we could add that, at the social level, it would undermine the process of social reproduction. Similarly, she notes that play in African tribal societies is an integrated part of life and occurs in the home, in the cattle camp or wherever the child happens to be, not in an adult-designated and bounded area. This example serves to underline the importance of the disintegration of social and economic life in technologically advanced societies. A product of the accumulation process is the separation and simplification of land uses, which on occasion brings children into conflict with adult interests and leads to attributions of deviancy.

It would be possible to add to the examples of muted groups reviewed in this chapter, but the object of the discussion is to demonstrate the essential similarities between social problems and associated environments, particularly, but not exclusively, urban ones. The examples I have cited all assume a political dimension, manifested in such forms as the feminist movement, debates on the merits of community care as opposed to institutional care for the elderly, policies to counter vandalism and so on. These social categories — women, children, old people — are recognized as distinctive yet integral elements of the larger society, but their distinctive needs are denied, misinterpreted or simply do not register. We could conclude that people formulating environmental and social policies, people working within hierarchically structured bureaucracies and other key decision-makers in the private sector, while adhering to a consensus view of society, are in practice strengthening boundaries between constituent social groups and thus, contributing to the concealment of different world-structures.

It may be appropriate to return to Bernstein's (1971) account of curriculum organization in the conventional British secondary school as a general model of the power structure in centralized systems. As he suggests, in representing the organization of the curriculum as a collection code, membership of a subject category is established at an early age, subject loyalty is fostered by teachers, and, with increasing socialization within the system, the differences between students of different subject loyalties becomes more marked, as do the differences between departments which become more concerned with internal coherence than with inter-subject communication. Strong boundary maintenance then secures vertical control. Significantly, Bernstein equates knowledge transmitted by a collection code with private property: 'This affects the whole ambience surrounding the development and marketing of new knowledge. Children . . . are early socialized into this concept of knowledge as private property. They are encouraged to work as isolated individuals with their arms around their work.' Without undue distortion, we could apply this scheme to the social formation, substituting dominated social groups for students with clearly defined subject affiliations and dominant capitalist interests and the government for the decision-makers in educational institutions. It is this power structure that is manifested in the compartmentalized built environment into which muted groups fit uneasily.

It would be unwise to push this argument too far in looking for analagous cases of dependency, discrimination and constraint that can be attributed to the practices of the dominant groups in society. There is a danger of ending up with what Rose and Hamner (1976) call a 'multitude of groupuscules', which could obscure the material basis of many exclusionary practices. Exclusion is clearly very pronounced in the case of some ethnic minorities because of their relationship to the means of production either as a part of the residual labour force or with a separate form of economic organization that draws its material resources from the dominant system, and a world-view that distinguishes them from the larger society. Where there is no ethnic difference the boundary is weaker because, unlike the ethnic minority that has an almost totally detached world-structure, dominated groups in the larger society are socialized into the dominant system and do not have the capacity to detach themselves. However, while we should be wary of superficial parallels, in the urban environment there does appear to be a consistent association of muted groups with 'left-over space' and a capacity to take over places nominally in the control of capitalists or the technocracy. One similarity between children and gypsies, as examples of muted groups, is that both demonstrate an opportunism in their association with the city, whether in the use of the street for skate-boarding or the use of derelict houses for stables and scrap breaking.

Conclusion

An explanation of the particular experience of one urban minority involves looking outwards to establish the relationship between the economy and social structure of the minority and the political and economic forces operating at the national or international level. Having approached the outsider problem from a comparative perspective at different scales, it has become apparent that, whereas the cultures of peripheral ethnic minorities vary, the response of the dominant society is unvarying and predictable. The same distortions are recurrent and stereotypes could be substituted for each other with little modification. I will use this concluding chapter to underline three features of the popular and official response which have more general implications for social science.

MYTHOLOGY AND THE BOUNDARY PROBLEM

It is notable that myth contributes in a significant way to the shaping of images of groups that do not fit the dominant social model. The possibility that the characterization of social groups like British gypsies may be based on myth is rarely considered, particularly in government circles, probably because these myths are functional — they serve to define the boundaries of the dominant system. Accounts of non-conforming behaviour assume the form of a romantic myth or they involve imputations of deviancy, which are also largely mythical; the romantic image, located at a distance or in the past, necessarily puts the minority on the out-side, while deviant behaviour, being polluting, also excludes. At the same time, the social system is recognized by politicians, the technocracy and other decision-makers as imperfect, containing within it groups that exhibit varying degrees of deviance, and, because society bears an imperfect correspondence to the model, there is a need for purification, manifested in practices designed to assimilate and integrate non-conformists. The purification process reinforces the boundary of the system, however, so that what is on the outside becomes more conspicuously different. I have sugges-ted that there is a spatial analogue for the purification process, demonstrated in the extreme case by designs for Utopia and, more generally, in the tendency to eliminate non-conforming land uses.

From the land use example, it is evident that the purification process can be connected, in Western industrialized societies, with the interests of property developers and industrial capital. In cities, one social consequence of this is that minorities that form part of the residual labour force or are considered extraneous to the dominant mode of production are relegated to marginal space, that is, to land that has not yet been incorporated in the primary economic system. Thus, we could suggest that pollution taboos that legitimate the exclusion of non-conforming minorities have a materialistic basis — they might be seen as a necessary defence for the accumulation process.

GOVERNMENT POLICY AND THE ANARCHIST
ALTERNATIVE

The imperatives of the dominant mode of production are faith-fully reflected in government policy towards outsiders, if not in stated policies. Thus, a government may pay lip-service to plural-ism, as in the British government's assurance that gypsies have a right to a nomadic life, but, in practice, it will attempt to regulate the minority. This is demonstrated, for example, by central government support for local attempts to restrict the movement of travellers and to exclude them from land that is wanted for any other purpose. Although these local exclusionary practices, to a considerable extent, reflect pressures from industrial and commercial interests, it is also pertinent to note that the minorities we are concerned with have little political power and that it is the interests of the electorate, including the working class, that are served by exclusionary policies. This complicates the issue. To the boundary between classes we have to add a boundary between the class-divided social system and the outsider. Furthermore, the boundary between the dominant system and peripheral ethnic groups is found under different political systems and, in particular, the response to outsiders in capitalist and socialist states cannot be distinguished.

Implicit, and occasionally explicit, in my account of the mainstream response to outsiders is the suggestion that a messier environment, with greater mixing of categories and the weakening of boundaries between social groups, would benefit peripheral minorities. If boundaries are weakened, the need for policing them is reduced and the state could become less involved in the regulation of society. This assumes that people are tolerant of diversity, but the actions of the state encourage intolerance, which is admittedly difficult to substantiate. The problem with this argument in the context of a capitalist society is that it is consistent with right-wing views on the furtherance of social justice, namely, that the market system will yield the maximum social benefits, ignoring the fact that the market system is a source of exploitation and inequality. I would argue, however, that it is not the fact of government involvement in social welfare that is the issue but the level of involvement. As I suggested in discussing the British government's policies for gypsies, to allow travellers to exercise their preferences in the use of land and to allow them unrestricted movement would make it possible for them to maximize their economic opportunities, and the allocation of land by the state rather than the allocation of sites should be sufficient. It is arguable that the provision of land that is accessible to urban markets and services would represent a greater redistribution of resources and would come closer to the pluralist ideal than would the provision of well-equipped sites in remote locations, accompanied as it is by constraining measures such as designation. This, of course, will not happen because it is incompatible with the demands of the capitalist system.

STATISTICS AND CATEGORIES

Data are generally desirable in social research, but concrete, factual information on peripheral groups must be treated with scepticism, partly because such groups are cryptic and elusive, making it difficult to obtain reliable statistical data on economic and social life, and partly because the collecting agencies are inclined to manipulate data for political reasons. The undercounting of British gypsies and the discounting of the native economy in assessing the living standards of the Inuit are, however, only blatant instances of a practice that is more general. It is apparent, for example, that comparative defence statistics are falsified in order to justify greater expenditure by the military establishment, and that accounting procedures employed in the production of trade statistics can be used to make a government's economic policy appear more successful than it is. If central and local government agencies distort or publish data selectively in order to provide support for a particular position, the production of statistics needs to be examined from an ideological standpoint.

More fundamentally, it is apparent from most attempts to describe the cultures of minorities that are as different from the social mainstream as the Inuit and travelling people that the economy and social structure are misrepresented because of the distorting effect of the categorical system. This can have important consequences for social policy demonstrated, for example, by the use of the term 'unemployed' in relation to peripheral minorities and the response that such a categorization suggests. The distorting effect of descriptive categories, while fundamental in the case of these minorities, is also a problem for the analysis of groups in the larger society, and we might interpret the interest in classification and coding, in fuzzy set theory and, more generally, in alternative syntactic forms as a recognition of the inadequacy of the conventional mode of categorization — that associated with 'normal' science. Because of the conformist tendencies that characterize most higher educational institutions, academics are not generally inclined to challenge a categorical framework that is seen as constituting the bedrock of acceptable knowledge. Thus, one possible benefit of working with social groups that are clearly beyond the bounds of the larger society is that, by attempting to understand the peripheral culture, we can develop a critical view of ourselves. If such introspection is to be profitable, however, we must be prepared to discard the conceptual equipment with which we are burdened by our education.

References

Acton, T. (1974). *Gypsy Politics and Social Change*. London: Routledge & Kegan Paul.

Adams, B., Okely, J., Morgan, D., and Smith, D. (1975). *Gypsies and Government Policy in England*. London: Heinemann.

Alexander, C. (1966). 'The city is not a tree'. *Design*, 206, 47–55.

Ardener, E. (1975). 'The problem revisited'. In S. Ardener (ed.), *Perceiving Women*. London: Dent.

Ardener, S. (ed.) (1975). *Perceiving Women*. London: Dent.

Armstrong, T., Rogers, G., and Rowley, G. (1978). *The Circumpolar North: A Political and Economic Geography of the Arctic and Sub-Arctic*. London: Methuen.

Association of Metropolitan Authorities (1974). *Minutes*, 10 December, Appendix A ('Sites for Itinerants'), p. 89.

Bachrach, P., and Baratz, M. S. (1970). *Power and Poverty*. Oxford: University Press.

Baker, T. J., and O'Brien, L. M. (1979). *The Irish Housing System: A Critical Overview*. Dublin: Economic and Social Research Institute, Broadsheet no. 17.

Barrell, J. (1972). *The Idea of Landscape and the Sense of Place, 1730–1840*. Cambridge: University Press.

Beadle, D. (1976). *Concrete Round the House*. Slough: Cement and Concrete Association.

Berger, J. (1979a). 'The peasant experience and the modern world'. *New Society*, 17 May, 376–8.

Berger, J. (1979b). *Pig Earth*. London: Writers and Readers Publishing Co-operative.

Berger, T. R. (1977). *Northern Frontier, Northern Homeland*. The Report of the Mackenzie Valley Pipeline Enquiry, vol. 1. Ottawa: Ministry of Supply and Services.

Bernstein, B. (1971). *Class, Codes and Control*, vol. 1. St. Albans: Paladin.

200

Bernstein, B. (1975). *Class, Codes and Control,* vol. 3. London: Routledge & Kegan Paul.

Booth, C. (1902). *Life and Labour of the People in London.* 3rd series, Religious Influences. London: Macmillan.

Bottomore, T. (1975). *Sociology as Social Criticism.* London: George Allen & Unwin.

Bourdieu, P., and Passeron, J-C. (1977). *Reproduction in Education, Society and Culture.* London: Sage.

Brody, H. (1971). *Indians on Skid Row.* Ottawa: Department of Indian Affairs and Northern Development, Northern Science Research Group.

Brody, H. (1973). 'Eskimo politics: the threat from the South'. *New Left Review,* 79, 60–70.

Brody, H. (1975). *The People's Land: Eskimos and Whites in the Eastern Arctic.* Harmondsworth: Penguin.

Brody, H. (1977). 'Industrial impact in the Canadian North'. *Polar Record,* 18(115), 333–9.

Brown, I. (1924). *Gypsy Fires in America.* Port Washington, New York: Kennicat Press.

Buttimer, A. (1979). 'Erewhon or nowhere land'. In S. Gale and G. Olsson (eds), *Philosophy in Geography.* Dordrecht: D. Reidel.

Caravan Sites Act, 1968, Part II (n.d.). A report of the Joint Working Party of the Local Authority Associations and the Gypsy Council.

Chesney, K. (1970). *The Victorian Underworld.* Newton Abbot: Readers Union.

Cohen, S. (1973). *Folk Devils and Moral Panics.* St. Albans: Paladin.

Cohen, S. (1980). Review of J. M. Moore, *Homeboys: Gangs, Drugs and Prison in the Barrios of Los Angeles* (Philadelphia: Temple University Press, 1979) in *Urban Studies,* 17(1), 86.

Connell, R. K. (1976). 'Planning for gypsies: aspects of current policies and practices'. Unpublished thesis for Diploma in Town and Regional Planning, Leeds Polytechnic.

Corrigan, P. (1978). 'Deviance and deprivation'. In P. Abrams (ed.), *Work, Urbanism and Inequality.* London: Weidenfeld & Nicholson.

Cotgrove, S. (1976). 'Environmentalism and utopia'. *Sociological Review,* 24(1), 23–42.

Crofton, H. T. (1908). 'Affairs of Egypt, 1892–1906'. *Journal of the Gypsy Lore Society,* 1(4), 359.

County Councils Association (1977). Minutes of the Planning and Transportation Committee, July.

Davidson, J. (1976). 'The urban fringe'. *Countryside Recreation Review,* vol. 1. London: The Countryside Commission.

Davis, J. H. (1977). 'Barrow, Alaska: technology invades an Eskimo community'. *Landscape,* 21(2), 21–5.

Department of the Environment (1976). *Accommodation for Gypsies.* London: HMSO.

Department of the Environment (1977 and 1978). *A Guide to Gypsy Caravan Sites Provided by Local Authorities in England and Wales.* London: HMSO. [The guide was modified for the 1978 edition.]

Douglas, M. (1966). *Purity and Danger.* London: Routledge & Kegan Paul.

Douglas, M. (1973). *Natural Symbols.* London: Barrie & Jenkins.

Douglas, M. (1975). *Implicit Meanings.* London: Routledge & Kegan Paul.

Dunleavy, P. (1977). 'Protest and quiescence in urban politics: a critique of some pluralist and structuralist myths'. London: Centre for Environmental Studies, conference on Urban Change and Conflict, York.

Elcock, H. (1979). 'Politicians, organizations and the public — the provision of gypsy sites'. *Local Government Studies*, May/June, 43—54.

Elliot, B. (1978). 'Social change in the city: structure and process'. In P. Abrams (ed.), *Work, Urbanism and Inequality.* London: Weidenfield & Nicholson.

Eversley, D. (1973). *The Planner in Society.* London: Faber.

Fincher, R. (1978). 'Some thoughts on deinstitutionalization and difference'. *Antipode*, 8(1), 46—50.

Foord, J. (1980). 'Women's place-women's space'. *Area*, 12(1), 49—50.

Foraie, J., and Dear, M. (1978). 'The politics of discontent among Canadian Indians'. *Antipode*, 10(1), 34—45.

Fraser, A. M. (1953). 'The gypsy problem — a survey of post-war developments'. *Journal of the Gypsy Lore Society*, 3rd series, vol. 32, 82—100.

Gentleman, H., and Swift, S. (1971). *Scotland's Travelling People.* Edinburgh: Scottish Development Department HMSO.

Giddens, A. (1976). *New Rules of Sociological Method.* London: Hutchinson.

Giddens, A. (1979). *Central Problems in Social Theory.* London: Macmillan.

Gmelch, S. (1975). *Tinkers and Travellers: Ireland's Nomads.* Dublin: O'Brien Press.

Gmelch, G. (1977a). 'Settling the Irish tinkers'. *Ekistics*, 257, 230—9.

Gmelch, G. (1977b). *The Irish Tinkers: The Urbanization of an Itinerant People.* Menlo Park, California: Cummings Press.

Goddard, D. (1972). 'Anthropology: the limits of functionalism'. In R. Blackburn (ed.), *Ideology in Social Science.* London: Fontana.

Gonzales, S. (1978). 'The white feminist movement: the Chicana perspective'. In K. O'Connor Blumhagen and W. D. Johnson (eds), *Women's Studies.* Westport, Conn.: Greenwood Press.

Graves, T. D. (1970). 'Personal adjustment of Navajo Indian migrants to Denver, Colorado'. *American Anthropology*, 72, 35—54.

Gregory, D. (1978). *Ideology, Science and Human Geography.* London: Hutchinson.

Gropper, R. C. (1975). *Gypsies in the City: Culture Patterns and Survival.* Princeton: Darwin Press.

Gurvich, I. S. (1978). 'Contemporary ethnic processes in Siberia'. In R. E. Holloman and S. A. Arutiunov (eds), *Perspectives on Ethnicity*. The Hague: Mouton Publishers.

Guthrie, G. (n.d.). *Cherbourg: a Queensland Aboriginal Reserve*, Studies in Applied Geographical Research. Armidale: Department of Geography, University of New England.

Habermas, J. (1976). *Legitimation Crisis*. London: Heinemann.

Harary, F., and Rockey, J. (1976). 'A city is not a semi-lattice either'. *Environment and Planning A*, 8, 375–84.

Hardin, G. (1968). 'The tragedy of the commons'. *Science*, 162, 1243–8.

Hardman, C. (1973). 'Can there be an anthropology of children?' *Journal of the Anthropological Society of Oxford*, 4, 85–99.

Harney, R. F., and Troper, H. (1975). *Immigrants: A Portrait of the Urban Experience, 1890–1930*. Toronto: Van Nostrand Reinhold.

Harvey, D. (1974). 'Class-monopoly rent, finance capital and the urban revolution'. *Regional Studies*, 8, 239–55.

Harvey, D. (1975). 'The geography of capitalist accumulation: a reconstruction of Marxian theory'. *Antipode*, 7(2), 9–21.

Harvey, D., and Chatterjee, L. (1974). 'Absolute rent and the structuring of space by governmental and financial institutions'. *Antipode*, 6, 22–36.

Hillier, B., Leaman, A., Stansall, P., and Bedford, M. (1976). 'Space syntax'. *Environment and Planning B*, 3, 147–85.

Honigman, J. J. (1973). 'Integration of Canadian Eskimos, Indians and other persons of native ancestry in modern economic and public life: evidence from Inuvik'. In G. Berg (ed.), *Circumpolar Problems: A symposium for Anthropological Research in the North*. Oxford: Pergamon.

House of Commons (1951a). *Official Report*, vol. 485, 20 March, 2280.

House of Commons (1951b). *Official Report*, vol. 486, 20 April, 2250–60.

House of Commons (1952). *Official Report*, vol. 498, 8 April, 2469–70.

House of Commons (1968a). *Official Report*, vol. 759, 1 March, 1919–2003.

House of Commons (1968b). *Official Report*, vol. 765, 24 May, 1154–79.

House of Commons (1969). *Official Report*, vol. 787, 23 July, 1988–2000.

House of Commons Standing Committees (1967–8). *Official Report*, vol. 6.

House of Lords (1968a). *Official Report*, vol. 293, 21 June 1020–55.

House of Lords (1968b). *Official Report*, vol. 294, 5 July, 583–634.

House of Lords (1969). *Official Report*, vol. 299, 13 February, 680.

House of Lords (1979). *Official Report*, vol. 398, 12 February, 1049–86.

Ingold, T. (1976). *The Skolt Lapps Today*. Cambridge: University Press.

Jacobs, J. (1961). *The Death and Life of Great American Cities*. New York: Random House.

James, W. (1973). 'The anthropologist as reluctant imperialist'. In T. Asad (ed.), *Anthropology and the Colonial Encounter*. New York: Ithaca Press.

Jones, D. (1974). *The Urban Native Encounters the Social Service System.* Fairbanks, Alaska: University of Alaska Institute of Social, Economic and Government Research.

Jorgenson, J. G. (1971). 'Indians and the metropolis'. In J. O. Waddell and O. M. Watson (eds), *The American Indian in Urban Society.* Boston: Little, Brown.

Kearns, K. C. (1977). 'Irish tinkers: an itinerant population in transition'. *Annals, Association of American Geographers,* 67(4), 538–48.

Knox, P. L., and Maclaren, A. (1978). 'Values and perceptions in descriptive approaches to urban social geography'. In D. T. Herbert and R. J. Johnston (eds), *Geography and the Urban Environment,* vol. 1. Chichester: John Wiley.

Koch, K. (1980). 'The new Marxist theory of the state, or the rediscovery of the limitations of a structuralist–functionalist paradigm'. *Netherlands Journal of Sociology,* 16(1), 1–20.

Kornblum, W. (1975). 'Boyash gypsies: shantytown ethnicity'. In Rehfisch, F. (ed.), *Gypsies, Tinkers and Other Travellers.* London: Academic Press.

Kornblum, W., and Lichter, P. (1972). 'Urban gypsies and the culture of poverty'. *Urban Life and Culture,* Spring, 239–52.

Kunitz, S. J. (1977). 'Underdevelopment and social services on the Navajo reservation'. *Human Organization,* 36(4), 398–403.

Lebas, E. (1977). 'Movement of capital and locality: issues raised by the study of local power structures'. London: Centre for Environmental Studies, conference on Urban Change and Conflict, York.

Levy, J. E., and Kunitz, S. J. (1971). 'Indian reservations, anomie, and social pathologies'. *Southwestern Journal of Anthropology,* 27, 97–128.

Maguire, M. (1974). 'Criminology and social anthropology'. *Journal of the Anthropological Society of Oxford,* 5(2), 109–17.

Marchand, B. (1979). 'Dialectics and geography'. In S. Gale and G. Olsson (eds), *Philosophy in Geography.* Dordrecht: D. Reidel.

Marcuse, P. (1977). 'The myth of the benevolent state'. London: Centre for Environmental Studies, conference on Urban Change and Conflict, York.

Marx, K., and Engels, F. (1968). *The German Ideology.* Moscow: Foreign Languages Publishing House.

Mead, M. (1978). *Male and Female.* Harmondsworth: Penguin.

Means, R. (1977). *Social Work and the 'Undeserving Poor'.* Birmingham: University Centre for Urban and Regional Studies, Occasional Paper 37.

Milan, F. A., and Pawson, S. (1975). 'The demography of the native population of an Alaskan city'. *Arctic,* 28(4), 275–83.

Miles, I., and Irvine, J. (1979). 'The critique of official statistics'. In J. Irvine,

I. Miles and J. Evans (eds), *Demystifying Social Statistics*. London: Pluto Press.

Miliband, R. (1969). *The State in Capitalist Society*. London: Weidenfeld & Nicolson.

Mingione, E. (1972). 'Urban development and social conflict: the case of Milan'. Paper presented to the International Sociological Association Research Committee on Urban and Regional Development Seminar; cited by Pahl, R. E. (1975), *Whose City?* Harmondsworth: Penguin.

Ministry of Housing and Local Government (1967). *Gypsies and Other Travellers*. London: HMSO.

Mooney, K. A. (1976). 'Urban and reserve Salish employment: a test of two approaches to the Indian's niche in North America'. *Journal of Anthropological Research*, 32, 390—410.

Munday, E. (1979). 'When is a child a "child" — alternative systems of classification'. *Journal of the Anthropological Society of Oxford*, 10(3), 161—72.

Neils, E. M. (1971). *Reservation to City: Indian Migration and Federal Relocation*. Chicago: University Department of Geography, Research Paper 131.

Nelson, H. J., and Clark, W. A. V. (1976). *The Los Angeles Metropolitan Experience*. Cambridge, Mass.: Ballinger.

Nisbet, R. A. (1969). *Social Change and History*. New York: Oxford University Press.

Novak, M. (1975). 'Subsistence trends in a modern Eskimo community'. *Arctic*, 28(1), 21—34.

Okely, J. (1975). 'Gypsy women: models in conflict'. In S. Ardener (ed.), *Perceiving Women*. London: Dent.

Okely, J. (1976). 'An economy on wheels'. *New Society*, 28 August, 468—70.

Okely, J. (1979). 'An anthropological contribution to the history and archeology of an ethnic group'. In B. C. Burnham and J. Kingsbury (eds), *Space, Hierarchy and Society*. Oxford: B.A.R.

Olsson, G. (1974). 'The dialectics of spatial analysis'. Washington, DC: Society for American Archeology.

Opie, I., and Opie, P. (1969). *Children's Games in Street and Playground*. Oxford: Clarendon Press.

Orvik, N. (1976). 'Northern development: modernization with equality in Greenland'. *Arctic*, 29(2), 67—75.

Oujevolk, G. B. (1935). 'The gypsies of Brooklyn in 1934'. *Journal of the Gypsy Lore Society*, 3rd series, 14(3), 121—7.

Pahl, R. E. (1977). 'Managers, technical experts and the state: forms of mediation, manipulation, control and dominance in urban and regional development'. In M. Harloe (ed.), *Captive Cities: Studies in the Political Economy of Cities and Regions*. London: John Wiley.

Pahl, R. E. (1979). 'Socio-political factors in resource allocation'. In D. T. Herbert and D. M. Smith (eds), *Social Problems and the City*, Oxford: University Press.

Parkin, F. (1979). *Marxism and Class Theory: A Bourgeois Critique*. London: Tavistock Press.

Parsons, G. F. (1970). *Arctic Suburb: A Look at the North's Newcomers*. Ottawa: Department of Indian Affairs and Northern Development, Mackenzie Delta Research Project, MDRP 8.

Parsons, T. (1961). 'An outline of the social system'. In T. Parsons, E. Shils, K. D. Naegele, and J. R. Pitts (eds), *Theories of Society*, vol. 1. New York: Free Press.

Pearson, R. W., and Smith, D. W. (1975). 'Fairbanks: a study of environmental quality'. *Arctic*, 28(2), 99–109.

Penzer, N. M. (1924). *Selected Papers on Anthropology, Travel and Exploration by Sir Richard Burton*. London: Philpot.

Pierce, J. E. (1977). 'Culture: a collection of fuzzy sets'. *Human Organization*, 36(2), 197–9.

Plummer, K. (1979). 'Misunderstanding labelling perspectives'. In D. Downes and P. Rock (eds), *Deviant Interpretations*. Oxford: Martin Robertson.

Public Health Inspector (1968), 'Discussion'. March, 293–324.

Rapoport, A. (1977). *Human Aspects of Urban Form*. Oxford: Pergamon.

Rea, K. J. (1976). *The Political Economy of Northern Development*. Ottawa: Science Council of Canada.

Roberts, B. R. (1978). *Cities of Peasants: The Political Economy of Urbanization in the Third World*. London: Edward Arnold.

Rose, H., and Hanmer, J. (1976). 'Women's liberation: reproduction and the technological fix'. In H. Rose and S. Rose (eds), *The Political Economy of Science*. London: Macmillan.

Rowles, G. D. (1979). *Prisoners of Space? – Exploring the Geographical Experience of Older People*. Boulder, Colorado: Westview Press.

Rowley, G. (1978). 'Plus ça change . . . a Canadian skid row'. *Canadian Geographer*, 23(3), 211–23.

Samuel, R. (1973). 'Comers and goers'. In H. J. Dyos and M. Wolff (eds), *The Victorian City: Images and Reality*, vol. 1. London: Routledge & Kegan Paul.

Savarton, S., and George, K. R. (1971). 'A study of historic, economic and socio-cultural factors which influence Aboriginal settlements in Wincannia and Weilmaringle, NSW'. Unpublished B. Arch. thesis, University of Sydney.

Sayer, R. A. (1976). 'A critique of urban modelling: from regional science to urban and regional political economy'. *Progress in Planning*, 6(3).

Scott, R. A. (1972). 'A proposed framework for analyzing deviance as a property of social order'. In R. A. Scott and J. A. Douglas (eds), *Theoretical Perspectives on Deviance*. New York: Basic Books.

Sennett, R. (1970). *The Uses of Disorder*. Harmondsworth: Penguin.

Smith, D. (1975). 'Irish travellers'. In B. Adams, J. Okely, D. Morgan and D. Smith, *Gypsies and Government Policy in England*. London: Heinemann.

Smith, D. G. (1975). *Natives and Outsiders: Pluralism in the Mackenzie River Delta, NWT*. Ottawa: Department of Indian Affairs and Northern Development, Northern Research Division, MDRP-12.

Stevenson, D. S. (1968). *Problems of Eskimo Relocation for Industrial Employment: A Preliminary Study*. Ottawa: Department of Indian Affairs and Northern Development, Northern Science Research Group, NSRC 68—1.

Sutherland, A. (1975). *Gypsies: The Hidden Americans*. London: Tavistock.

Taylor, P. J. (1976). 'An interpretation of the quantification debate in British geography'. *Transactions, Institute of British Geographers*, n.s., 1(2), 129—42.

Thomas, D. K., and Thompson, C. T. (1972). *Eskimo Housing and Planned Culture Change*. Ottawa: Department of Indian Affairs and Northern Development, Northern Science Research Group, Social Science Notes 4.

Tipps, D. C. (1973). 'Modernization theory and the study of national societies'. *Comparative Studies in Society and History*, 15, 199—226.

Turner, J. F. C. (1976). *Housing by People*. London: Marion Boyars.

Usher, P. J. (1972). *The Bankslanders: Economy and Ecology of a Frontier Trapping Community*. Ottawa: Department of Indian Affairs and Northern Development, Northern Science Research Group, 71—1, 71—2, 71—3.

Usher, P. J. (1976a). 'Evaluating country foods in the Northern native economy'. *Arctic*, 29(2), 105—20.

Usher, P. J. (1976b). 'The class system, metropolitan dominance and northern development in Canada'. *Antipode*, 8(3), 28—32.

Ward, C. (1976). *Housing: An Anarchist Approach*. London: Freedom Press.

Ward, C. (1978). *The Child in the City*. London: Architectural Press.

Ward-Jackson, C. H., and Harvey, D. E. (1972). *The English Gypsy Caravan*. Newton Abbot: David and Charles.

Worrall, D. (1979). *Gypsy Education: A Study of Provision in England and Wales*. Walsall: Council for Community Relations.

Yates, A. B. (1970). 'Housing programmes for Eskimos in Northern Canada'. *The Polar Record*, 15(94), 45—50.

Index